MY CONFESSIONAL

BOOKS BY HAVELOCK ELLIS

MY CONFESSIONAL

Questions of Our Day

BY
HAVELOCK ELLIS

Boston and New York
HOUGHTON MIFFLIN COMPANY
𝔗𝔥𝔢 ℜ𝔦𝔳𝔢𝔯𝔰𝔦𝔡𝔢 ℌ𝔯𝔢𝔰𝔰 ℭ𝔞𝔪𝔟𝔯𝔦𝔡𝔤𝔢
1934

The Riverside Press

CAMBRIDGE · MASSACHUSETTS

PRINTED IN THE U.S.A.

CONTENTS

MY CONFESSIONAL

I

MY MAIL–BAG

IT is my fortune — whether good or bad I am not always sure — to receive many letters. They come from the most varied parts of the world besides Europe, from China and New Zealand and the heart of Africa, and above all from most of the United States, Washington down to New Mexico. Some of them, of course, are from old friends parted by the chances of life; some are from friends who have grown intimate though never seen; others, perhaps the largest number, from complete strangers.

Of these a considerable proportion are of a kind most authors sooner or later become acquainted with: 'I am sending two of your books which I shall be delighted if you will autograph, with the quotation in each of some favourite passage from your writings. I should also like to have a photograph of yourself, inscribed to me, which I can frame. Please also give me a brief summary of your views on the immortality of the soul. And what is your definition of God? And kindly describe your methods of work, for I should like to be able to write as you do.'

I hasten to add that this is a composite picture of a large group of letters, for not more than two or three of these requests usually occur in a single letter.

Authors have sometimes bitterly complained of such demands, and of the weary task of packing these books for return and trudging along with parcels under each arm to the post-office perhaps more than a mile away. I remember the fierce indignation of my friend Olive Schreiner, who suffered much from ill-health, at the frequent burdens of this kind which were put on her, and I recall especially her mischievous glee over some most expensively bound copies of her books for the return of which she had ignored all requests, though I expect she may have relented at last. Another indignant author (Martin Armstrong) professes to have written a letter to his butcher on the pattern of those he thus receives, eulogising that craftman's skill in the art of butchery, asking him to explain how he acquired it, and suggesting that such admiration might well be rewarded by the present of a piece of steak and a pound of sausages. The steak and sausages, Mr. Armstrong claims, duly arrived, accompanied by a bill, but the letter failed to evoke any sympathetic reply.

It is not, however, with that class of letters that I propose to be occupied here. I receive them meekly, not without a smile, never with a curse, and to a large number I send some sort of an answer, ultimately, sometimes at so wide an interval that the writer, if still alive, must have long ceased to expect any reply. There is another class of letters, equally large, of a different order, even, it might be thought, smacking of the confessional. It is these that will chiefly come before us here.

That word 'confessional,' let me say, is not here used with any thought of calling up the ecclesiastical associations of the term, or even the modernised form of it sometimes supposed to be psychoanalytic. There are not only confessions of 'sin,' demanding penitence and absolution, but also confessions of 'faith.' The confessions that come to me are of both kinds, and even wider still. They have this in common with those that come to the priest and the psychoanalyst that spiritual intimacy is required with a minimum of physical contact. We have all doubtless admired the ingenuity of the Catholic Church in the construction of the confession box, though when personal confession was first introduced in the fifth century it was no doubt under such simple direct conditions as I can recall as a child on the voyage to Australia, when the steerage passengers before Easter came one by one into the little cabin of the Bishop of Bathurst — an admirable Irishman long since dead — and knelt at his feet as they entered. Even more informal and intimate is the attitude my correspondents feel able to assume when speaking at a distance of often many thousand miles.

Their confessions, while sometimes indeed of sin, often very mistakenly as I am able to give the assurance, and sometimes of faith, are frequently of still another class which I may call self-affirmation. That is to say that the writer, shut up in an uncongenial atmosphere of office or home or boarding-house, unable ever to be his or her real self, feeling that below the surface of affection even parents or wife or husband are strangers, seems suddenly for the first time to hear a voice that speaks simply and directly to the 'soul' as it used to be called. The stifled self utters a responsive cry, seeking in its turn to be heard, and to assert what is hidden within, mere truisms often, it would seem to some of us, though in many circles unutterable. After a varying interval — it may be almost instantaneous, it may be of ten years — a letter is timidly written and with much misgiving mailed. When an answer arrives the recipient is sometimes therewith content, and makes even no acknowledgment. Sometimes, on the

other hand, a correspondence of ever-increasing intimacy results. In one such case I have received as many as one hundred and fifteen letters in twelve months, from a very distant
correspondent who has here for the first time spoken with an
inner voice, and they have all been of interest.

That my own share in such a correspondence has been far
smaller I need scarcely say. But I never feel that I ought entirely to disregard the letters of this class. I never willingly
throw them aside. Even, however, if the answer is brief, it
often needs thought, especially when a complicated situation
is presented for consideration. I have asked myself whether
I am justified in disregarding the advice and the practice of
my friends by the attention I thus give to my miscellaneous
correspondents. I do not in the end usually feel much doubt
about the answer to that question.

If, however, it should ever seem a mistake to give to a few
what might be given to many, there is a method by which my
conscience could be soothed. I am here undertaking to adopt
it. I propose to select some points from letters that have
reached me and discuss them if not in the directly personal
way in which I have actually written to my correspondent, at
all events in its essential impersonal point. Tangled histories
and tragic situations will not come before us, for my correspondents must remain completely anonymous. The
points that appear may yet be found endlessly varied. We
shall meet many of the chief questions of our day.

II

THE NATIONAL PREJUDICE

AN American friend, a dancer and teacher no longer young in years but full of energy and spirit, is accustomed to wander, during vacation, searching for strange folk-dances in the more remote districts of Europe, whence now and again she writes to tell me of her adventures. My friend's keen mind is occupied with many things outside her own field, even including politics. Now she sends me an American newspaper which criticises the English Government. 'You may not like it,' she says, 'but you ought to know what is said on our side.'

I am not troubled by the criticism. In a democratic country where the government is determined by the votes of the citizens, that government may represent but a small majority of voters, and even sometimes, by a sudden revulsion of popular feeling, a minority. So that there is ample room for criticism of a country by the country's citizens themselves. For my own part, I can say that, if ever I vote, the candidate I vote for nearly always comes out at the bottom of the poll; it can seldom happen that any government represents me. Like a large proportion of my fellow-countrymen, I am no more responsible for the policy of my own country's government than I am for that of the United States.

For the most part, however, it seems not so much governmental policies as personal attitudes which arouse these national recriminations. A native of one country always tends to find, or to fancy that he finds, a critical if not disparaging attitude in the native of another. He is often right. The only comment to be made, and it is decisive, is that here he is up against the general human characteristic, universal though quite superficial, to be critical of what is not like oneself. All children show it; one sees it indeed most pronounced in that alarming person, the average boy. In every boys' school the boy who is a little unlike his fellows quickly acquires a nickname to mark the distinguishing trait. For persons of another nation this tendency becomes generalised. When I was a boy at school every Frenchman was a *Froggie* and every American a *Yankee*. I should add that while there was a touch of contempt felt about the 'Froggie,' as being not only a person presumed to be able to live on frogs (an ancient tradition, for Tilly tells us that in the eighteenth century even an English peer believed that all Frenchmen lived on frogs) but also inheriting the character of a national enemy through many centuries. There was no corresponding feeling with regard to the 'Yankee,' for the periods of hostility between England and the United States were too brief to leave any trace on the national memory. And the whole attitude was abstract and not concrete. It so happened that our headmaster in this English school near London was of French descent and his wife an American, yet there was never, however privately, any belittling whispers on this score among us about either of them. It has always seemed to me that the people who take too seriously this natural tendency of the youthful mind — and so many adults remain youthful — do not themselves deserve to be taken too seriously.

When we put the matter on the national basis which here comes before us, of England *versus* the United States, we

have but to take an impartial attitude to find the supposed
opposition dissolving. If England contemplates America
what it is facing is itself, only more so. Certainly sometimes
much more so. When from the outside the Spaniard
Madriaga lately compared America with England, a chief
difference he found was merely that Americans have a
greater tendency than the English to admire and absorb
the civilisation of France. But even that is merely one of the
more so differences. England had, again and again, in
spite of all hostilities, been profoundly influenced by France;
and it was Sir Philip Sidney, himself fighting against France,
who sang of that 'sweet enemy.' England was a very thor-
ough 'melting pot' long before the term was invented for
America. If I try to recall the names of the Presidents of
the United States (I make no claim to recall them all),
most of their bearers were doubtless hundred per cent
Americans, but they present an almost unbroken array of
unmistakably British names. The English kings, on the
other hand, are often foreigners, sometimes imported direct
to the throne from abroad, and even unable to speak the
English language, while, as for the spirit of revolution, that
was English long before it was American, and the English
have again and again crushed, exiled, or executed their
rulers. Landor, himself a representative Englishman, long
ago coupled Washington with Cromwell, and certainly
Washington was a more typical Englishman than Lord
North.

An American journalist wrote to me to protest against my
statement that most of the Presidents of the United States have
borne British names. Some of their names, he declared, are Irish.

I tried to explain to him that 'British' is the only inclusive adjective we possess to cover the natives of our Islands generally. I should myself like to see 'English' accepted for nominal use in this extended sense, just as 'French' is used to cover all the various peoples gradually united with an originally small country. But whenever it is so used, a protest is sure to arise from some native of the northern part of Great Britain who will probably describe himself as 'Scottish,' though his greatest fellow countrymen of old were proud to call themselves 'Scotch,' and may have considered 'Scottish' too nearly skittish. Fortunately the Welsh do not yet describe themselves as 'Walish.'

The native of the United States is no better off for adjectives. He cannot call himself 'United Statish' or a 'United Stateser.' He has to fall vaguely back on 'American,' which may mean Canadian or Mexican, and many other things besides. The great Thomas Paine, who baptised the 'United States' when scarcely yet born, had not provided for this contingency.

III

IS SEX NECESSARY?

WILL you kindly give me a little knowledge,' writes an unknown correspondent from Springfield, Massachusetts, 'on the biological, social, moral, and eugenic reasons why I should love a woman?'

I have not answered that question, and I do not propose to. My correspondent has not told me anything whatever about himself, and the answer might be, 'There are none.' But at the same time I am pleased to know that such questions are being asked, and not only at Springfield, Massachusetts. For it is not long since the appearance of the learned treatise: *Is Sex Necessary?*

In the years when I first began to occupy myself with the problems of sex, nobody ever asked that question. It was always taken for granted that there was no occasion for such a question. If we go back to the Middle Ages, it was still assumed that there was no place here for discussion, even though the answer to the question might be in the negative. You went into a monastery because you knew that the state of chastity is holy, or you stayed outside and married because you knew the Divine Command to increase and multiply. That injunction, 'Be fruitful and multiply,' is still repeated even today by those who forget that it was addressed to a world of some eight people and is out of place in a world of much over eight hundred million people. Moreover, it is a command that was addressed not only to Man but to all living things, the influenza germs, for instance, which have so faithfully followed the divine command (for the moment, though only for the moment, I speak as a Fundamentalist) that during the Great War they were able to destroy even more of the human beings obeying the same command than the War itself destroyed. Under latter-day circumstances there is evidently not only a Divine Command but a Divine Warning, which now at last we begin to hear.

So it is that my correspondent's question marks a turning-point in human history. I say in history, not merely in individual lives, because the fate of nations rests ultimately upon questions of sex. Even unconsciously it does so. The Protestant Church which claimed for its clergy the right to marry was not thinking of the race or the nation. But in the end it has appeared that the clergy, who in a celibate Church would have been sterilised, have procreated in most of the Protestant countries a larger proportion of the men of light and of leading, for their nation and for the world, than any other social group.

Today we may approach these questions consciously and deliberately; we may discuss the solutions; we may even begin to carry them into practice. We study psychology and psychoanalysis and whatever they seem to teach us regarding the indulgence and the repression and the sublimation of sex, in order to be able to adjust or to readjust our personal relationships in or out of marriage. We have learned to take into account the economic factors of life, and to know that even if we believe that God provides for our children, it is we ourselves who are responsible for the instruments by which this provision is effected. We are beginning to learn — so far only beginning — that not all members of the human race are fitted to carry on that race, and that it is our business to exert the social pressure which will ensure that this consideration becomes a guiding motive in life. At the same time we seek to make it possible that those who are inapt for racial ends are guaranteed a reasonable well-being and happiness in the pursuit of higher personal or social ends. The command, 'Increase and multiply,' has become modified into 'Decrease and Improve.'

A distinguished French thinker argues that primitive man was not guided by reason in the same manner as we are guided (or supposed to be guided), but lived in a pre-logical world of thought. It seems to me very doubtful. But at all events we may say that, before today, human beings certainly lived in a pre-logical world so far as marriage and parenthood are concerned. They followed instinct or else they obeyed supernatural commands, which might be either positive or negative. Today we have placed these questions on a natural and realistic foundation, and everyone now feels free to ask himself: 'Is sex for me necessary? And if so, how so?' A revolution has been effected which may alter the whole constitution of the race.

The spirit that stirs in Springfield, Massachusetts, is slowly covering the world.

IV

AN OPPONENT OF EUGENICS

A BRILLIANT and sympathetic young American friend is preparing himself for the career of medicine at a famous European University. His letters, often touching on new points of medical advance, are instructive, and written in expectation of a congenial reception. Today, perhaps in a mood of depression, he has become a little aggressive and he writes attacking my advocacy of eugenics. The problem, he declares, may be clear, but not its solution, and if eugenics is directed to eliminating the stupid people, it will be robbing us of a valuable and necessary part of the community; moreover, if successful in this, there would still be a relatively stupid section of the community acting as a burden on the rest, and I might myself come to be regarded as belonging to it. There is enough intelligence in the world as it is, he concludes, if properly applied, without introducing any new eugenic principles, provided the intelligent would work to screw up the stupid to a proper pitch of idealism. Let us make the best of the world as it is!

I am not setting out to defend eugenics. Nowadays there are plenty of people to do that. I would only remark that I have never had any hostile feelings to stupidity, being far too conscious of my own, and that I do not regard eugenic practices, if not eugenic principles, as new, since they have been carried out from the days of early Man, even though by methods we now consider barbarous; it is simply a question of maintaining them in forms more suited to our own state of civilisation. But I am not now proposing to discuss these points.

Only a few days before my correspondent's letter arrived, it chanced that I had come upon an early essay of my own, published when I was still much of the same age as my friend is today. In it the subject of eugenics is casually mentioned. The mention is neutral. But I found that on the margin I had pencilled after publication: 'I don't believe in eugenics.'

I noted that comment with surprise and amusement. I also found in it much cause for reflection. We seem so easily to forget our old selves. May it not often be that the views we advocate today were the views we had no faith in on some long forgotten yesterday? No doubt, when that is brought home to us, we may claim that our opinions have changed because the circumstances have changed. A minister in the English Government, long conspicuous for his support of Free Trade doctrines, has just introduced a tariff measure; and when taunted by an opponent for having expressed entirely different opinions a few months ago, he calmly replied: 'What I said in June and July was quite right in June and July.' But there is more in it than that.

Schopenhauer said that, whichever path we take, there is that within us which could only be satisfied by following the opposite path. We finally choose the path which seems the more fully satisfying, but we cannot pursue it in peace unless we forget the possible delights of the opposite path. That is where Freud's Unconscious comes in. We let drop into that abyss the discarded self it would be inconvenient to remember. The consequence is that when we meet the

119745

man who has chosen the other path, instead of greeting him affectionately as our other self, we look at him as a stranger and an enemy.

We do not always allow our rejected self to fall so quietly into the Unconscious. I often recall the fine distinction which Huysmans made between letting fall and flinging away. We let fall what we regard with calm indifference or judicial rejection. What we violently fling away has its roots in our own hearts, which is why so fierce an effort is needed. When I note that an eminent musical critic cannot refer to Tchaykowsky without a sneer or to Wagner without disparagement, I feel convinced — apart from any estimate of either composer — that in his earlier developments the critic was once a Tchaykowsky fan and a devout worshipper at the shrine of Wagner.

So that I bear my correspondent no ill-will for his derogatory remarks on what I now consider the highly important question of eugenics. There must be something in the opposition to eugenics: I shared it myself. When I see the opponent of eugenics go by, I can say: There, but for the grace of God, goes Havelock Ellis.

V

THE WORLD'S FUTURE

A CORRESPONDENT who knows that I am interested in the subject, calls my attention triumphantly to an article in the November *Forum*: 'Birth Control: What is it doing to America's Population.' I had already read the article, which is by the President of the American Public Health Association, who is also Statistician to the Metropolitan Life Insurance Company; he speaks with authority. It is worth while to consider the picture of the future he presents.

In 1990, it is here estimated, the American population will reach 154,000,000 and that will be its maximum before decline begins. Even that estimate may be 'too optimistic,' since urbanisation and rationalisation will accelerate the movement. So we may more probably expect a birth-rate of 10 per 1000 by the year 2100, with a highest maximum population of 148,000,000 in 1970. Supposing the birth-rate falls to 10 per 1000 there will be only 21 per cent of the population under twenty years of age, but 40 per cent over the age of fifty, a population far more largely than now of middle-aged and elderly men, in this respect 'unduly weighted.' The atmosphere, we are told, will be much more sober and conservative than now, and old women will become unduly influential. 'A very disturbing picture indeed could be painted.'

I do not accept our distinguished statistician's pessimistic views even if his figures may be accepted as possible, apart from his failure to realise that the whole world, whether or not more slowly, is marching along the same road as America. It is in the first place hazardous to picture a future world moving exactly at the same rate as the world we happen to inhabit at the moment. One need only recall that, so far as we can ascertain, the world's population during hundreds, even thousands, of years has increased so slowly as to be often almost stationary. The sudden spurt that began during the eighteenth century and attained such an extraordinary impetus that, in the United States for instance, it was once possible for the population to be doubled in twenty-five years, can only be regarded as a temporary lack of balance certain to become adjusted again, with or without conscious social control.

What we witnessed during the last century was a new and incalculable increase of human power over the processes of Nature, leading to an immense increase of production — mechanical production and human production alike — without any corresponding increase in the control of that production. What we witness in the present century is the result of that disorganised production: In some regions wheat and cotton and rubber and coffee are left to waste and even positively destroyed, while, in other regions the whole population are languishing or even starving for lack of those products which they cannot afford to buy. So also the human products, here subsidised by short-sighted rulers so that even their feeblest specimens may be aided to propagate and survive, there swarming under such evil conditions that they are always liable to be swept away by famines and floods and plagues. We cannot too much admire the skill of the nineteenth century mind in gaining so marvellous a power over Nature, in devising new instruments of production, in discovering the methods of combating disease, securing hygiene, and making possible longevity. But we must not assume that therewith the human mind will stand still. There remains for the twentieth century the task of stabilising this productivity, of building up the necessary system of international control by which alone population and subsistance can be brought into a state of harmonious equilibrium all over the earth. That will be a result not less glorious than the result achieved by the century behind us, and will still only be a beginning. There are more fields beyond to conquer.

But how about a future 'overweighted by the elderly?' I have heard before about this terrible prospect. Do those who shudder at it realise that the century of intense vitality and movement out of which we spring — a century not only full of wild adventures in the physical world but of startling social revolutions — was more 'overweighted by the elderly' than any that preceded it? Even if we contemplate single conspicuous figures, we do not always find that the men who are reaching four score reveal a less eager radicalism than those of younger generations. We may even refuse to tremble at the future large contingent of elderly women; in the past, it is true, their influence may sometimes have been unfortunate, but that is simply because in youth they were shut out from sources of social development which to their daughters are open. I refuse to be alarmed over the 'sober conservatism' of the old women whom today I know in youth.

Indeed it seems to me that those who express these fears are blind to the world they live in. Our world today — which is constantly becoming a more elderly world — is being created anew. Conceptions of life and society, more radically novel than have ever stirred widely on the earth before, are becoming realised before our eyes. We have but to look at the Revolutions of Germany and Russia and Spain, all of them — with India and China in the same path in their wake — in various ways seeking to carry into practice fruitful germs which were generated elsewhere, even in England and the United States, though in their places of origin they develop more slowly, and, as we hope, more effectively. This is happening in a world that, we are solemnly assured, is becoming more and more dominated by 'sober conservatism!' Surely I may safely refuse my correspondent's invitation to quake even before the *Forum's* eminent statistical pessimist.

VI

HILDEGART

I AM a girl, my age is sixteen, and I am Spanish, three things which I expose first as my recommendation to you.' So writes a new correspondent from Madrid in fluent though not always correct English. The statement may arouse no surprise, though still it is not usual so to hear from Spain. But wait!

My 'sincerely true friend and pupil,' as she finally calls herself, proceeds in a matter-of-fact way to tell me that she has just qualified as a lawyer though not yet of age to practise in public, that she is now working at philosophy and medicine, having selected these two additional professions to study, during the three years' interval before attaining the legal age, and that she also proposes to visit other countries, especially England, to ascertain their laws and customs. She has been a Socialist since the age of fourteen and is largely concerned to spread enlightened views among the workers of her country. This she does by delivering lectures, by journalism in the popular press, and by writing books. She has published numerous books in popular style and is engaged on a large one 'which is now finishing itself.' Her books are on eugenics, sexual education, and birth control. She sends me one on 'The Sexual Revolution,' written in a clear, orderly, precise way, straightforward and simple and vigorous. She advocates such reforms — all new to Spain — as co-education, Lindsey's companionate marriage, health-certificates before marriage, free divorce, maternal clinics, child guidance clinics, birth control, sterilisation of the unfit, with a number of other like reforms. In advocating these radical measures, which she does with all the confidence and conviction that youth today finds scope for in the more advanced countries, she shows herself extraordinarily well-informed as to what is being proposed and carried out on these lines in other countries, especially England and the United States. It is the desire to gain yet further information on these matters which leads her to write to me.

I have long been a devout admirer of the women of Spain. More than twenty years ago I discussed the fine qualities which, at the best, they have proved able to display. They have often seemed to me of finer quality than the men, and I could understand how it was that a great dramatist of old Spain could employ the idea of 'virility' in a non-sexual sense, and bestow it on a woman as freely as on a man. Women in Spain have for long past come naturally to the front in all progressive movements, even when — as under conditions that have only lately ceased to exist in Spain — that involved much daring and some danger. In old days women in Spain possessed many rights which placed them in a better position than European women generally possessed, and, at all events in substance and spirit, they were able to maintain it in spite of the pressure upon them of the Spanish Church and the Spanish State and Spanish society with its semi-Oriental views of feminine seclusion. I ventured to foretell that when at last the pressure of this atmosphere was removed 'Spanish women will play their part in directing the civilising influences of the twentieth century.' All the same, this Spanish girl takes my breath away. She passingly mentions that she is considered 'valiant.' Yet even in the land of Don Quixote she seems too extravagant to be real. If it were not that she writes in so simple and matter-of-fact a way I should be tempted to think she must be a magical illusion, and that life really is, as the Spanish poet long ago declared, a dream.

It happens by a coincidence that I receive today a query from a young American woman: do I think, she asks, that the younger generation of our time will contribute good material to the world? Well! if it should come about that one per million of that generation proves able to face the world with the spirit and the equipment of my young Spanish lawyer (I am not assuming that the proportion will actually be so large) I have little fear about that generation.

Alas! the hopes here expressed were destined to be crushed by a sudden and tragic event. For two years I was in constant friendly correspondence with Dr. Hildegart (as she became) whose activities as a writer in popularising sexological knowledge, as a lecturer, and as organising secretary of the Spanish branch of the World League for Sexual Reform grew ever more conspicuous. Then, without warning, and before she had attained the age of nineteen, Hildegart was shot in her sleep by her mother. The mother and daughter, as I knew, had been devoted to each other and were inseparable even in University classrooms. Hildegart was an illegitimate child, and the mother, Doña Aurora Rodriguez, a woman of most remarkable character and ability, regarded her daughter as her own sole creation, and as the mouthpiece of her own ideas and aspirations. This absorption and the resultant jealousy at last reached a morbid and insane pitch.

VII

BETTY'S BABY

BETTY had already been inspired to write to me once or twice in rather a general way. Then she wrote to ask my advice; she was expecting a baby, her second, and had gone into a Nursing Home conducted on radical lines, fruitarian and so forth, but it proved so dirty and ill-organised that Betty felt she could not possibly produce her precious baby under such conditions: What would I advise? Betty, you may guess, is 'modern'; her domestic life seems to be largely led in a caravan with which to wander about the wildest parts of the country; she is a Rationalist in creed but with a temper of joyous vitality, revelling in all forms of Nature, and never happier than when sleeping out under the stars, or throwing aside all her garments. Walt Whitman is perhaps her chief hero, and it may have been only into the second letter I received from her that she slipped, together with a picture of her first child, a photograph of herself standing naked by a mountain stream in Scotland, a lithe taut slender figure with firm little breasts, in spite of maternity and her thirty-five years.

My advice was simple and emphatic. Have nothing to do with any Maternity Homes of that kind, which are almost certain to be bad, for faddists are seldom capable of carrying out even their own cranky ideas: go to the most ordinary and commonplace Home you can find; it is fairly certain to be at least clean and well-conducted. She thereupon bravely moved into the Maternity Ward of the general local public Infirmary of the town near which the caravan happened just then to be planted, and was astonished to find it so much more satisfactory than she would have anticipated. Baby was in due course born ('just like Daddy') and Betty was happy.

But one thing worried her, and that was the conversation of the young mothers, women of the people, in the Ward where she lay. 'My heart has ached at the conversation around, suggestive jokes on sex, and remarks on the predominance of boys born; "I wonder why they are all boys." "There must be going to be a war." "Yes, they are needed in a war." "Expect there will be another in twenty years time." My soul revolts at such complacency. How many per cent mothers talk thus of war as inevitable in the scheme of things, instead of preventable? I felt like crying out: "I do not breed sons to be butchered!" But some of these mothers were Catholic or bigots, so I held my peace, though I felt like bursting. What can I do to help the cause of enlightenment? Oh! the world in itself is so beautiful — and spoilt by lack of knowledge. If only I could do something!'

I commended Betty's self-control — which I did not regard as cowardice — for there is a time to speak and a time to be silent. One defeats one's own ends by not observing those times. Yet the question remains.

It really brings us up to a fundamental problem which is not even yet viewed alike by all: the problem of whether it is desirable to avoid war. We may all perhaps agree that in primitive times war was an admirable invention — an invention because it is scarcely ever found in the animal world and certainly not in the family from which Man sprang. It was a method, and practically the only available method in early days, of achieving the social organisation and the collective discipline without which civilisation would not have been possible; quite apart from its value, which primitive women so highly appreciate in their men, of fostering courage, strength, endurance, resourcefulness. And if, as even until lately in some parts of the world, the battle was brought to an end when but a single fighting man was disabled, and both sides thereupon fraternised, the victors paying, by way of consolation, an indemnity to the conquered side, the evils of war were minimised. Today, as we know, war is another matter, and, if we think of it, much less beneficial, for we have other and better ways of attaining social cohesion, and as for personal qualities there is no scope for their cultivation when the soldier by no will of his own is merely a necessary little cog, easily replaceable, in a huge machine, often directed against an invisible foe and by methods liable to destroy combatants and non-combatants, women and children, indiscriminately. 'An Ancient Virtue and a Modern Vice' was the title my wife gave to an article written during the Great War. Today war is not only degraded but unnecessary; in every civilised state we have known how to provide a national police force to meet the risk of individual citizens murdering each other. If we fail to take the next obvious step of setting up an international police force to meet the risks of nations murdering each other we meet the fate we deserve, for our civilisation not only stultifies itself but grows stagnant and corrupt. We have failed to grasp the fact that mankind is becoming a single unit, and that for a unit to fight against itself is suicide.

So I tell Betty that, though as an individual she may do little, as a social being, in a world where there are just now not only too many hard hearts but far too many soft heads, she can, merely by virtue of being herself, and showing that she is herself at every fitting moment, in thought and in word — not to mention her vote as a citizen — do much. Perhaps most of all she may do much by so bringing up her child that his mentality will not be that of those who built up the world of today. As she herself writes: 'He must draw in wisdom and knowledge with his milk.'

VIII

THE PLACE OF SENTIMENT

A LITERARY agent in Paris reports to me that he has not been successful in negotiating a translation of my book *The Dance of Life*, as French publishers seem to fear it would be too sentimental for their public.

That opinion caused me surprise, and a little amusement. It contrasted so strongly with the charges I had for many years been accustomed to hear brought against the work of one who, it was sometimes declared, had in the most outrageous manner torn away the veils of sentiment to reveal the actual facts of life. But at all events this new charge restored what personally I regard as a wholesome balance. If I am a realist I do not feel that I have therefore thrown away sentiment, for sentiment is itself a substantial part of the reality of life. Lately I was visiting a show of landscapes by the English painter Algernon Newton and observing how well in art this great truth may be realised. Here was an artist who accepted the bald and precise facts with the vision of a Canaletto, and yet, one felt, was a poet in the same sense as Claude. Or, if we turn to a greater and more famous painter, in Rembrandt we find the closest, the most ruthless, even sometimes the crudest realism, not merely associated but interfused with an emotional expressiveness as intense as in art has ever been attained.

There can be no doubt that among that post-war generation which is now passing away there was a shrinking horror of everything that could, rightly or wrongly, be called 'sentiment.' All sentiments seemed to them illusions, and mischievous at that. When the war fell on the world they had been possessed of all sorts of shallow and fanciful notions about life which the war shattered. But instead of thanking whatever gods they might still believe in for a deliverance from the bondage of dreams, and firmly resolving to build up the world on a better foundation, they could only moan over their lost delusions. It was pleasanter to find fault with the world than with their own folly. They were, as someone has put it, 'broken-hearted because they have no hearts.' They had lost their old sentiments only to put on a still more peculiar sentimental equipment.

A little psychology might have led to a clearer vision. At the very period of the war Alexander Shand was putting forward his memorable work, *The Foundations of Character*. Essentially that work is a study of the sentiments, that is to say the highest and most complex system of the impulses, appetites, desires, emotions, and passions which mark us as human beings. To modify a man's sentiments is to modify his whole character, for every sentiment is the organisation of a part of his character, and often an elaborate part, standing in a dynamic relation to his whole effective personality in the world. Every man is a group of sentiments, even though of meanness and of greediness and of cynicism. It is so that his habits are formed, and habits create what is characteristic in him. 'The qualities of sentiment are the qualities of character.' The difference is not in their absence but in their quality and in the degree of their strength. A friend once told me that his wife, a highly intelligent woman, had been reading some volumes of my essays and had come to the conclusion that my distinguishing characteristic was passion. The idea seemed new to me, but, though I hope that reader's insight had seen what was not too obvious, I never resented the sentimental imputation.

'We want blood, Mrs. ——, we want blood!' So, I have been told, James Hinton once vehemently exclaimed, flourishing the carving-knife, at the head of the family dinner table. That man of restless vitality and pioneering genius was not expressing any cannibalistic cravings; it was passion that he meant, the dynamic sentiments needed to live more fully, and to leave the world richer than we found it.

Today, when we are perhaps witnessing the disappearance of a rather languid and anæmic generation, I have sometimes echoed Hinton's words. When I look at many a man still alive among us I cannot help sadly reflecting that when he comes to die (I hope by a natural death) no Lady Macbeth will be likely to exclaim: 'Who would have thought the old man to have so much blood in him!'

IX

THE SIGNIFICANCE OF THE DANCE

PHYLLIS is studying at a University in the Far West. But it is a dancer she wishes to be, and she desires so to plan all her activities that they may be directed towards that goal. She belongs to a family that has travelled much about the world, and she is prepared to plan the approach to the desired profession on a large scale. She now writes to ask my advice. 'Is it better to study, closely or from afar, all the dancing of the world, and to try to take from it the qualities which make it fine, or is it better to dance, as Orozco paints, from immediately surrounding life? To be an eclectic and glean from the whole world, or to trust to one's own immediate civilization? Shall I go wholeheartedly into the dancing of the Wigman school, let us say, or from the dance of life everywhere work out a dance which is *my* life?'

Before such a problem, as may be guessed, I can only reply that no abstract solution is possible. It entirely depends on Phyllis herself, on her own aptitudes, her own tendencies, not to mention her own special opportunities. But I will not dwell on my reply to the question since I do not claim any technical knowledge of dancing. I wish here to say why it is that, nevertheless, I feel entitled to take a deep interest in dancing.

There is, first of all, the fact, which I have so often tried to make clear, of the typical and symbolical significance of the dance in our whole cosmic and human world. As Sir James

Jeans, one of our chief authorities where speculation on the make of the universe is concerned, has remarked: 'The motions of electrons and atoms resemble those of the dancers in a cotillion.' And if we turn from Nature's art of design in the so-called inorganic world to our own organic human world and to our own art in design, the same resemblance is found. A distinguished English art critic who is also himself an artist, D. S. MacColl, has lately declared that 'drawing is at bottom, like all the arts, a kind of gesture, a method of dancing upon paper.' He means that it must have its measure and its harmony in itself, and be complete in itself; it is not mere imitation, even when a mimetic element is present. That is what the dance is, and to hold the idea of the dance before us is a wholesome check on our imitative artistic tendencies as on our metaphysical divagations. It is on a pattern of measure and balance and harmony that our life must be lived if it is to be well lived. Yet there is more in it even than this.

Yesterday I went to the first production of the Camargo Society. This is a Ballet Society, recently formed in London with the object — now that with the death of Diaghilev and other causes the inspiration of the Russian Ballet is spent — to gather together and develop whatever fine influences in dancing may be found. They seek the collaboration of the best available composers, painters, and choreographers in the production of classical and original ballets, and already number among their active members many eminent representatives of those arts.

As at moments I sat entranced before the spectacle on the Savoy Theatre stage, a conviction which I have sometimes experienced before arose within me anew. The dance is more than a mere symbol, however great the significance it as such possesses. It is the dance, and the dance alone, which brings out in full measure all the essential and fundamental properties of the human organism: its delicacy and its strength, its intelligence and its skill, brain and body working together in the achievement of beauty through the very substance of the human animal. A Shakespeare or an Einstein, and many an athlete, may overwhelm us by some special prodigious manifestation of strength in art or intellect. But here alone we may properly exclaim: What a miracle is Man! The dance is the final justification of Man, and the justification of whatever Power it was that made Man.

X

THE EONIST

SEVERAL letters have reached me from unknown correspondents with regard to a sentence of eighteen months' imprisonment with hard, labour lately passed on a young man at Leeds Assizes. The report of the trial is not so clear as it might be, though the newspapers describe it in the largest type as 'amazing,' and the judge seems never to have heard of such a case before. The charge, which was of 'indecency,' set forth that this youth, Augustine Hull by name, had for six months past dressed as a woman and during that period been courted by another young workman whom he agreed to marry, though before the wedding day he disappeared, thus inflicting on the would-be bridegroom what the judge denounced as 'a cruel wrong.'

My correspondents, shocked at the sentence, wrote to me because they knew that this anomaly was not so amazing as the judge and the journalists supposed, and that I have written of it at length. It is an anomaly which in Germany is called Transvestism or cross-dressing, but which I term Eonism, because much more than cross-dressing is involved, and the mental disposition may exist without even the wish for any change of dress. The name Eonism indicates an origin from the Chevalier d'Eon, who was the most noted representative of this anomaly more than a century ago and played a conspicuous part in European history and diplomacy as the trusted agent of Kings and statesmen. His actual sex

was at the time disputed, but he was really a man who pre-
ferred to live as a woman, and so, in old age, he died in
London. These people are frequently, like the Chevalier
d'Eon, of high character and distinguished ability, normal
in other respects, often devoted husbands and affectionate
fathers. But they would rather be mothers than fathers,
they feel like women, they share the tastes of women, and
most of them, not all, delight to indulge, when they can do
so without detection, in the refinements of the feminine
toilette. At the present time I know one such who for considerable periods, both in America and in England, has
lived as a woman, with a woman friend who is in the
secret, leading an entirely decorous and honourable life;
dressed as a man, he appears normal, robust and masculine;
but as a woman he never betrays his sex, and is indeed said
to be more like a woman, more 'ladylike' in his ways, than
the average woman.

Augustine Hull is evidently a more radical example of
this anomaly. He is a simple workman, a colliery haulage
hand, belonging to a very poor family. But from early
childhood he felt like a girl, he played with girls' toys, and,
as he grew older, was accustomed to do all the feminine
tasks of housework. He takes girls' parts at theatricals; it
gratifies him to wear women's clothes and he feels at home
in them. More than that: even in male costume he looks
like a girl, is slight and feminine in build, and with a feminine voice. So much is he like a girl that at the age of seventeen when returning from Church one Sunday morning in
ordinary male attire he was arrested by the police, taken to
the station and stripped because he was supposed to be a
girl masquerading as a man.

To all well-instructed people the case is simple. It was evidently so to the two medical witnesses who were called, one a psychoanalyst and the other the prison surgeon. But their evidence went for nothing. The judge pronounced his sentence of eighteen months' hard labour and when the case was carried to the Court of Appeal the judge of that court dismissed the appeal in a few brief remarks which concluded with the statement that he 'did not consider the sentence a day too much.'

In Germany and some other countries of the Continent of Europe a more reasonable attitude towards the eonist tends on the whole to prevail. It is beginning to be acknowledged that a genuine taste for cross-dressing, whether in a man or in a woman, providing that it leads to no public disturbance of order, is not properly a matter for police interference. There is a tendency for the police to view it with tacit acceptance, and medico-legal experts have even argued that police permits should be issued in these cases, valid during good behaviour. It is stated that the two countries in which the harshest and most antiquated attitude towards the eonist still prevails are England and the United States. That is my reason for bringing forward the matter here.

Four centuries ago in the city of Basel a cock was solemnly tried and publicly burnt alive in the market-place for the unnatural crime of laying an egg. Today we know that there was here nothing unnatural. Sex depends on the balance of the hormone-producing glands, and that balance sometimes results in states that are naturally inter-sexual. We now understand this when cocks and hens are concerned. We shall some day understand it a little better where our fellow-men are concerned. Until then it might be as well to avoid treating them in the spirit in which our ancestors treated the cock that laid an egg.

It was Magnus Hirschfeld of Berlin who first described cases of Eonism in detail, terming the condition 'Transvestism' or cross-dressing, and putting forth a book on the subject in 1910. I had already been interested in such cases and was inclined to term the condition 'sexo-æsthetic inversion.' But that term seemed misleading, and later I devised that of 'Eonism' and devoted a lengthy study to the matter in Volume VII of my *Studies in the Psychology of Sex*, 1928. The objection to the term 'Transvestism' is that the psychic condition involved may exist apart from any impulse of cross-dressing.

The Chevalier d'Eon de Beaumont was born in Burgundy in 1728 and died in London in 1810. Numerous books have been written about him, both in French and in English.

XI

THE FATE OF THE PROLETARIAT

IT has taken me more time than I like to admit,' writes a valued correspondent whose work is in sociological fields, 'to assimilate your idea that the proletariat is approaching extinction, now, at the very moment its triumph is being proclaimed. Of course you are absolutely right. Now that you have pointed it out to me, I have discovered the reason for many contradictory impressions I gathered in the U.S.S.R.'

My friend goes on to remark that, with her American background, it is rather a shock to her to realise that the sympathy she had developed for the various plausible means of relieving social oppression have been given to a matter which was, after all, not fundamentally important. I hasten to comment that, on this point, I am by no means in agreement. On the contrary, it is that active sympathy which has aided, and is hastening, the future disappearance of the proletariat. Economic causes are of course the prime factor, but that factor can be helped or hindered by the social attitude, and according as that attitude is, or is not, actively sympathetic, the transformation of the proletariat is effected by mild methods of evolution or cruel methods of revolution. In any case, however, it is effected. And if an economist of genius had arisen a century ago he might have foreseen what today we see.

But why is it still so difficult to see, even for those who, like my friend, are familiar with scientific economics? The

reason, I think, is that our vision is so often clouded by emotion. Our sympathies themselves have handicapped us.
We have surrounded the proletariat with a halo of romance.
These dumb, oppressed, inarticulate workers at the base of
our social structure — how they have appealed to all our
generous emotions! How they have excited all our aspirations for a new and better world! 'The future belongs, whatever happens, to the proletariat!' exclaims Nicolas Berdyaeff,
carried away by the ideals of the Bolshevists while con-
demning their methods; 'it is inevitable, it is just!' I can
recall, as a youth, talking with an English worker, then old,
who had been crippled for life by being sent as a child to
work in a factory. He viewed his fate calmly, as an economic
necessity that could not have been avoided. The resentment
which I felt — I who had never done a day's work in a
factory — he was unable to share. So it has always been.
The glorification of the proletariat has been the work of
the middle class. Every movement to stir the proletariat
has had a bourgeois leader. Karl Marx is the supreme type,
a student seated in the library of the British Museum, con-
sumed by enthusiastic zeal on behalf of the proletariat, and
altogether remote from the actual economic facts of the
developing proletarian situation.

For what are these facts? The proletariat means, as the
name signifies, that lowest stratum of a population which
possesses nothing beyond its prolific ability to produce offspring. More precisely, it is the class of those who have
hands to work and children to replace them, but no other
form of capital. In certain social stages a very useful class,
whose cause deserved championing. But — it will happen!
— the moment when the triumphant champions of a cause

appear is the moment when the cause itself is melting away.

Today we do not want more or less unskilled hands, because we have ever more perfected machines which will do their work, and for delicate manipulation need no mere proletarian but a skilled worker. Standardisation, rationalisation, and careful selection of personnel are the three great industrial factors of today, and they are totally incompatible with the existence of a proletariat. Thus in England we have the National Institute of Industrial Psychology working along these lines, applying the principles of the Industrial Health Research Board, and active in vocational guidance. In one factory, for instance, they have made it possible for four girls to maintain the output which had previously required eleven. That is what is happening everywhere. So that in every 11,000 workers, 7000 have become superfluous, unwanted members of the community. Moreover, this is only the beginning of what is possible with the growth of knowledge and investigation. Again, a large sewage disposal scheme is now being established near London. Everything will be done by machinery, and a task which thirty years ago would have needed some 1500 men will now be accomplished by about thirty, assisted by the power represented by 1,500,000 units of electricity. The regiment of navvies formerly needed were proletarians: the small group now needed will be skilled and highly paid workers. It may easily be seen that, even at the present rate, before many years have passed there will not be a single proletarian left in England. Or, if there is, he will be placed in the Zoölogical Gardens or otherwise carefully tended. And in the United States he will probably have disappeared at an earlier date.

This brings us to another aspect of the matter. When the Romans invented the word, they especially thought of the proletarian's productivity of offspring. In their days, when the population was small and not tending unduly to increase, that was a not undesirable aptitude. It is quite another matter in an overcrowded world, and when every country is doing its best to keep people out. In a community of unrestricted individualists where the maxim prevailed: 'Every man for himself and the Devil take the hindmost,' there would be nothing to say against unlimited procreation. But in our civilisation that maxim is not accepted. We have put ourselves in the Devil's place and taken charge of the hindmost. Our society, that is to say, recognises a certain responsibility for its members. And if it is responsible for maintaining them when once brought into the world, that means that it must assume control for bringing them in. Society cannot accept responsibility for those of its members whose entrance into the world it has not sanctioned. We profess the contrary; we put up a fine bluff. But we know at heart that this is the core of the situation.

Meanwhile, we keep alive the unemployed remnants of the great proletarian armies of old. We either put them on the dole or we exercise charity. For in one country they like to feel they have a legal right to a dinner, and in another country they like to regard it as a gracious gift. It comes to the same thing. Indirectly, one way or another, in the end they will both alike have to pay for it.

XII

IN THE PLACE OF WAR

A SWEDISH doctor writes that he agrees with the opinion I have expressed that Death and Pain are essential elements of Life, absolutely necessary for human development, and he also agrees that war is not now the best form of Death and Pain to assume. 'But,' he asks me, 'what on earth shall we put in the place of war?'

It so happens that precisely the same question has at the same time been asked by Dr. L. P. Jacks, a distinguished teacher, in England. Here in the current *Hibbert Journal* he writes at length on the problem of 'The Moral Equivalent of War.' Dr. Jacks, it must be noted, is not a militarist who has set out to beat the pacifist down; he has signed a petition for the reduction of armaments; he believes in the eventual abolition of war. But, he feels, a nation's army and navy have hitherto alone given us that disciplined co-operative courage without which no organised society can survive. He knows of no other social service with a disciplined training expressly to meet death and pain, the merchant service being, as he well says, the nearest approach. It is because the League of Nations has not attained that level, he remarks, that it still remains weak; and no doubt, if some machinery could be devised for executing a certain percentage of its adherents the League would quickly become immensely more powerful in the world. Jacks is not impressed by the solution of this problem which William James long ago put forward, though he thinks that politicians would legislate better if they had previously done some years service in James's army of dish-washers, and the Labour-leaders be wiser for a training in the army of bankers.

To me James's idea of a disciplined army to fight against Nature fails to appeal for rather different reasons. There is something artificial, I would say, in setting up discipline in opposition to Nature, since discipline is part of Nature, and life in Nature would collapse if it were not maintained by a perpetual discipline. And there, perhaps, is a clue to the solution of the problem. The great and varied tasks of civilisation which await us today offer endless possibilities of courage and discipline and organisation — even in the fight against war — if we are to breed a race of fine citizens, trained in body and mind to face these tasks; and with the warlike traditions of the race behind us the necessary new forms of discipline will arise spontaneously. Even without war there are endless chances of fighting pain and death.

I must confess, indeed, that I have never myself been able to take this problem very seriously. For two reasons. In the first place, as so many people still fail to realise, war is not a primary aptitude of mankind or a habit of the stock from which Man arose. If it had been, one cannot well see how all these difficult and delicate acquirements by which man distinguishes himself from the other animals could ever have been devised or cherished or developed, since man is so defenceless an animal and with so prolonged an infancy. All his energies were needed for constructive purposes and there was little left over for destruction. The early implements of man are tools; an incalculably long period elapsed before weapons were thought of, and it was during that vast period that the lines of human progress were for ever laid down. There is, says an authority on early man, 'no evidence whatever for the existence of war during the period of early man. Economic conditions were vastly different and the ruling motives for war absent. Human nature has no inherent disposition to warfare.' Indeed it might be said that weapons came in as luxuries, scarcely before metal was used, and together with other luxuries. That does not mean that armies and navies performed no useful purpose. It is certain that they did, and were a powerful factor in social organisation, heightening the energy and efficiency of concerted human activities. They have long ceased to do so; the conditions are totally different; they have even become different since the last great war.

There is, however, another and still more decisive consideration. All those virtues of courage and heroism and discipline and organisation which may once have been there are absent from the stupendous mechanisation of warfare today. It is still not commonly known that the next war, if ever it comes about, will attain an intensity of which the last great war can give us no conception. There was lately published a book which has been soberly described as 'the most terrible book that has ever been written.' It is an enquiry, organised by the Inter-Parliamentary Union at Geneva, entitled *What Would be the Character of the Next War?* and its authors are a score of experts — soldiers, chemists, engineers, physicians, psychologists — who for the most part write in a precise and technical spirit. They acknowledge the futility of defence against attack. Aircraft can now be controlled by wireless and, even if brought down, explode their full death-dealing discharges, including flames that no water can put out and blistering dew of which three drops are fatal; a single bomb can destroy a whole city block and penetrate any subterranean shelter. A couple of machines might suffice to wipe out a city of the size of London, and the whole population of a country, men, women, and children, could be practically destroyed even before the actual armies had any opportunity of meeting. The war would end before it had begun. Under such conditions heroism and discipline mean no more than they could mean for the inhabitants of Pompeii who, whether they faced the stream of lava or fled from it, were alike overwhelmed. The moral would seem to be that armaments are of all methods the worst for obtaining that 'security' which governments are always prating about. They never seem to understand that along this line, whatever they do, their neighbours will go one better. Yesterday it was announced that even little Belgium has ordered from an English aviation company sixty of the latest and best type of bombing machines, so that the blessings she received in the last war she may distribute to others on a more deadly scale in the next great war.

When that comes about I picture how the pacifist of today, who had spent his life preaching in vain, will lean over the golden bars to gaze down at the scene on earth, and (when no angel is within earshot) mutter to himself: 'Serve 'em right!'

XIII

THE GENIUS OF FRENCH ART

A STRONG will, or an incessant preoccupation with will-power (which I take to be the basis of all ethics), being inhibitory and also destructive, is the enemy of æsthetic sentiment, which is exhibitory and creative, or, in the passive form, appreciative.' So writes to me a subtle critic whose special field is music, but is here trying to cover art generally. Art, he holds, is attained when the free play of the finer senses is allowed to serve as a channel of well-being (euphoria, to use a more technical term) for the natural flow of our energies, if no subconscious prejudices are allowed to restrict that flow. He admits that prejudices are sometimes inevitable, and that, for instance, the lovely play of sunshine on a golden heap of manure may thus fail of its due æsthetic effect. There seems to me an important element of truth in this statement. At the same time it may be possible to push the statement further.

I have just been to visit the Exhibition of French Art during seven centuries now being held at the Royal Academy of Arts. I was careful to arrive at the moment of opening for the day, when it is possible to stroll through the whole series of empty rooms and absorb an impression which the presence of a crowd would obscure or obliterate. Certainly, even for one who enters with large expectations and some knowledge, it is a magnificent show. One imagines what a delight it must have been for the Committee of French and English curators of Galleries to form for once a beautifully balanced presentation of all the phases of a great national art, and to omit whatever might injure the total effect. In the indiscriminate wealth of the immense Louvre no such immediate overwhelming impression is possible.

The impression is at first of a singular sensitiveness and receptivity in the face of the visible world. In this art the world is represented more nakedly, more intimately, than we are accustomed to see it represented. At the beginning this receptivity was most manifest in the aptitude to be influenced by the art of neighbouring peoples, especially in the Netherlands and in Italy, for at the outset French painting was not clearly distinctive, whence it comes about that experts still dispute whether some notable early paintings are French or English. The architecture of France had reached a climax of perfection when painting was still in swaddling clothes, which it only cast off in the fifteenth century. But from the first we may observe this sensitiveness, notably in delineating human expression with a natural vivacity which even startles us if we have in mind the hieratic or conventional types of expression in Italian and other modes of early art. It is really the same quality of sensitive and intimate contact turned towards the face of Nature which — more perhaps than any actual love of Nature — made French artists pioneers in landscape painting; and Claude Lorrain is for many people the foremost among them. Here, with little doubt, we have that free and direct play of the senses, with the inhibition of ethical and other prejudices removed, which my correspondent regards as the foundation of art.

But that hardly seems enough. In French painting, at all events, I have seen more than that. All through I see the tendency — alternating with or combating or blending with that sensory awareness — to make a pattern. This is really a form of that love of logic which we are always finding in the French. It appears in many forms: in the love of a hierarchic social order, in philosophic systems, in the rhetorical formality of French verse, even in the famous etiquette of French politeness. We see this love of pattern showing itself in crude and too obvious ways in the earliest of distinctively French paintings. Throughout, it is this tendency which seems responsible for that mannerism and conventionality and self-conscious affectation which is the besetting weakness of French art where it falls away from its summits. But on the higher level, this tendency to pattern — to rhythm and harmony and balance and measure — is part of the great quality of French art, the quality which has made the French supreme in architecture. It is revealed in painting, and at an early period, even in single figures, notably at first in sculpture, and so well maintained throughout that it may be with surprise that a woman bathing by Renoir somehow instantly recalls a statue of a fourteenth-century saint one has just seen in another room. And in Poussin, the first great French master of composition in painting, we find this instinct for pattern wrought to its highest point, and becoming a dominant impulse for artists who came after, yet always in conflict or in balance with that direct and intimate feeling for the sensory contact that one noted first.

We find throughout the course of French painting this conflict of opposing influences — each tending sometimes to push back the other, both tending sometimes to meet in harmony. Because of it French painting has become a supreme manifestation of art. No single impulse could suffice; it is only on the two wings of their rhythmically balancing impulses that the summits of art have in French painting been reached.

The painter's art reflects human life. Whether in the experience of the individual or social groups, it is in the harmonious rhythm of conflicting impulses that the vital tension is maintained, the onward and upward movement ensured.

XIV

THE GOETHE CENTENARY

IN view of the centenary of Goethe's death the editor of a London weekly has asked me to write an article for the occasion.

I have never written about Goethe. It is a vast subject, well fitted for contemplation it has seemed to me, none more so, but hard to write about. When my first book, *The New Spirit*, was published many years ago, a reviewer who was, I believe, the poet Henley, declared that Goethe, that 'colossal sentimentalist' as he called him, stalked through the whole volume. If anyone except myself is to stalk through my books, there is no one I would be more proud to see doing it than Goethe, though, as a matter of fact, I had scarcely mentioned Goethe's name.

But note my critic's description of Goethe, the 'colossal sentimentalist,' for that brings us to one of the main troubles about Goethe: he is so big that everyone may find him the embodiment of what he supremely dislikes. The invalid Henley, fully justifying Adler's doctrine of the 'masculine protest,' naturally found in Goethe the representative of the sentimentality he had set himself to hate. The Bohemian artist, on the other hand, despises Goethe as the perpetual Prime Minister of a petty state (even if the size of Athens) and taking in hand all its manifold practical administrative details, though these activities were not only highly beneficial for the community but brought that close touch with life the artist needs. The modern debunker views with de-

spair the calm Olympian figure displayed with never a
vulnerable spot in his armour by Eckermann (fine artist as
he was, that disciple knew how to build up a picture), while
the old world critic deplores the wild adventures of the sin-
ful young realist who had not yet become an Olympian.
For the Classicist Goethe is an extravagant Romantic, and
for the Romantic a frigid Classicist. His scientific equipment
and discoveries do not possess significance for the specialist
who disdains amateurs, though that is what many of the
finest men of science have been. The patriot despises
Goethe's internationalism, his love of France, the enemy
of his own country. His novels, no doubt, fail to appeal to
the readers of Arnold Bennett and Sinclair Lewis, or his
lyrics to the devotees of T. S. Eliot and Edith Sitwell, while
the profound philosophy of life packed into all the seams of
his work usually escapes notice altogether.

So it comes about that no one has ever written well of
Goethe, and no biography of him ever gives much satisfaction save to the man who wrote it. An exception which
some seem inclined half-heartedly to make is in favour of the
Life by G. H. Lewes which by a happy chance came first
and was the work of a many-sided amateur who was not
over weighted by all the data which have been piled up
since, for we can now follow the history of Goethe almost
day by day for a great part of his life. There is perhaps no
one indeed whom we may know so intimately on all his
sides. That is the difficulty: everyone who approaches him
can only see what he himself likes or dislikes, and everyone
else sees something different, often something exactly opposite.

That is not only the difficulty, it is also the significance of Goethe. Now and again a man has appeared in the world who has seemed universal, a lover of all things. In an earlier world Leonardo da Vinci was such a man. Goethe was the latest of these immortals and the most complex, the most many-sided. That was necessary to make him the man of our time. Carlyle, himself by no means a true Goethean man, was yet a true prophet when he wrote a century ago, on Goethe's death, that there was in his books 'a new time' and added: 'The cornerstone of a new edifice for man is laid there.' It is still true. There is nothing in us which we may not find already in him, and in a more harmonious synthesis. He includes not only our faiths but also our scepticisms and our cynicisms and even our obscenities. Not only in our inner world is he with us, but also in our outer world; engineering feats (as at Suez and Panama) then only dreams, which we have achieved, he had foreseen. He reveals indeed our weaknesses and defects, yet he was sensitively alive to the influences of life and nature and art, fearless in accepting all, ever the supreme dilettante, which means in the deepest sense the lover, the great master of life.

We cannot think about Goethe too much: it may be wise not to talk about him, and he himself said that the deepest things are not for speech. So I have briefly replied to my friend the editor that I regret I cannot accept his invitation to write on the Goethe Centenary.

XV

MAKE ROOM FOR THE PIONEER

A CORRESPONDENT writes from Washington, D.C., that he has seen the statement attributed to me that the pioneer spirit is a need of mankind today. He is eager to know more about this. 'I am twenty-five, a recent college graduate, single and ready for hell. But I cannot go in search of it because the world frowns on a man who does not stick to the God-awful business of increasing his salary and making a public-conscienced citizen of himself.'

So, while sitting behind a desk in an office at a salary which will increase in time, if he meekly follows the direction of his elders, he longs for adventure. But what, he asks, should he do? There is the police force, but it is not considered just the thing, and, besides, there is nothing adventurous in bawling out traffic orders. There is the army, but no spirit of pioneering independence is fostered there. A job on a steamer? But that means all sorts of formalities which merely tighten up one's shackles. In politics, again, adventure is called 'radicalism' by the elder men of the group who have a slave-hold on the younger man of ambition. So he ends up: 'How? When? Where? Who?'

I have not replied to my correspondent. He belongs to the large class of people who may day-dream of adventure but are not of the stuff of which adventurers are made. Adventure would cease to be adventure under the conditions which he demands. He will probably make a good and estimable citizen, and had better continue to sit behind his desk and work towards that increased salary which, when the present depression has passed, he may receive. The world needs many such men as he, but at the moment it may perhaps hurt his feelings to tell him so.

The world also needs a few men of a totally different type. Indeed at present it could perhaps do with a fairly considerable number, since through the excessive timidity and tremulous caution of its rulers, paralysed in attitudes of impotent obstinacy, it sometimes seems in danger of stagnation. There are men who, unlike my correspondent, do not fear to move unless they are backed by what a former editor of the London *Times* has just now disrespectfully termed 'a prosperous fat-bellied humanity composed of poltroons.' These men are prepared to leave that feeble crowd behind their backs — and even the prospect of an increase of salary — for the love of adventure is in their blood, and the difficulties that involve danger and a spice of risk do not drive them back but draw them on. They know that in the end, when the danger is past, the feeble folk behind will pluck up heart and follow them, and even fall at their feet.

There never was an age with so great a scope for adventure as ours. Great pioneers have, it is true, appeared now and again in the past. A Columbus has arisen here and there and led adventures which have had immense consequences. But in the years since most of us were born an era of adventure has opened. In every spiritual and material field we are pushing beyond the known into the unknown, carrying the torch of science to disperse the gloom around us, harnessing the great forces of Nature to our own small forces for the immense magnification of our power over the world, penetrating, as none ever penetrated before, into the obscure mysteries of the mind, planning for practical realisation schemes of social reorganisation which of old were merely the dreams of philosophers or the abortive struggles of madmen. In all these fields, even those that are counted most spiritual, it is the pioneer who comes first, the man who can face risks, carry his life in his hands, and be willing to lose it even at the hands of those whom he desires to redeem. The pioneer of today may well be forgiven if he sometimes finds tame and futile the adventures of old, whether on the battle field or on the mission field.

But adventure can only come to the adventurous, though it may come to those who, unlike my correspondent, have never longed for it, but when it comes have shown that they possess the temper of the hero. For its coming cannot always be foretold. 'How? When? Where? Who?'

XVI

THE DISCIPLINE OF PAIN

THE inevitable has happened after great suffering,' writes a friend who is a physician, and also a psychoanalyst, a few days after the death of his wife. 'The only consolation I have is that she has at last peace. Seeing her immense agony has not reconciled me to any theory of pain. It seems to me that pain is nothing but the crude imperfection of this life on earth. It has to be borne, but seems to have no compensatory virtue.'

I have offered no other consolation to my friend. But I am touched by this simple and natural utterance as coming from one of whose profession it is a chief part to find remedies for the pains alike of the body and the spirit. I am far from accepting his statement, but this is a matter which has a personal aspect and an impersonal aspect, sometimes hard to reconcile, and at the moment my correspondent is too overcome by the personal aspect to be able so much as to see that there is an impersonal aspect.

On that aspect nothing seems clearer than the beneficent character of pain. To take a potent and typical source of pain: fire. It is a proverbial saying that a burnt child fears the fire. All men who work near furnaces are liable to excruciating and sometimes fatal accidents. It is sad. But if that were not so, all life might long ago have been licked up by flames. And fire, as the proverb itself indicates, is merely a symbol of the dangers by which we are ever surrounded. Our whole life is conditioned by the possibility of pain.

It is the danger signal which concentrates our attention on the point at which our existence is at stake unless we are alert, even though sometimes all our efforts may be in vain. No pain, no life. So that if we come to the conclusion that, on the whole, life is good, that is a roundabout way of saying that pain is good. Pain is the guardian angel of life.

The same position is revealed if we turn from the material side of life to its psychic side. All living things are perpetually haunted by the fear of pain, for the fear of pain is but another aspect of the love of life. In a sense that is true even of plants, however unconscious it may be in them, for all the actions of plants could be intelligibly accounted for by such a fear. With animals, as we know, it is a main guiding motive of life, however far removed from man, and there is nothing animals learn so quickly as a new fear, which means a new presentiment of pain. We often hear how in regions of the world remote from human aggression animals at first peacefully accept the approach of man, and how very quickly they know better. The higher apes in no way show more clearly their superiority and their nearness to man, than by the fact that their daring in the advance to better methods of living is accompanied by a complex of cautious fears. If life may be fittingly described as a dance, that means that it is a tense system of varied movements amid risks, a sword dance with an inevitable sword also suspended above. The dance is joy because it is also discipline, the exaltation of a skilful triumph over the latent possibilities of pain. Therein is the compensatory value of pain which my friend just now fails to see.

There are solid easy-going people in the world who seem to have had a minimum experience of pain; at a distance they may pass for healthy animals, peaceful shell-encased limpets firmly glued to the rocks of life; but they have missed the best that life can give. The people I have known who have most exquisitely tasted the joy and rapture of living are those who have known most of its discipline of pain. All life is on the foundation of discipline. To fail in life means to be unable to accept that fact and to face it courageously. For life is little if not heroism, and all living things are martyrs.

Is this attitude optimistic or pessimistic? Bertrand Russell, a penetrating yet sympathetic critic, declares that I am an optimist. It may be so. But there are optimists and optimists.

XVII

THE HISTORY OF ALICE

IT is some years now since Alice first wrote to me, timidly and vaguely. I encouraged her to be more precise. In her next letter she wrote: 'For about twelve years now I have suffered great mental torture as a result of something that happened when I was a child of about twelve years of age. For several years after it happened, it passed from my mind, but when I began to realise the beautiful things of life I began to feel myself unclean and then the torture began.'

The incident was trifling, quite innocent, the harmless inquisitive action of a young brother to which she had consented. It may happen in any family and makes no impression when a healthy atmosphere prevails. It made no impression on Alice, as we see, until six years later. But she had been born into a poor and ignorant home in the East End of London, where some subjects were concealed in an impure shame, and silence and disgust were falsely counted Puritanic. It was only when Alice came to know the existence of this attitude that her own sense of impurity began.

'When I first realised how horrible it was (when about eighteen years of age) I thought I would go mad and knocked my head against the wall in a frenzy of distraction. These periods of mental suffering occurred frequently and became an obsession. I always avoided having boy friends because I felt I must not marry.' From her parents Alice could receive no help. Her father was a bricklayer, a keen Socialist who spent all his spare time preaching Marxian doctrines at street corners; her mother was a domestic slave who soon wore herself to death. 'I then suffered again badly. A man fell in love with me and suggested marriage. I did not feel that I was fit to marry anybody. In my agony I felt I must rush away somewhere. I went to France. There a man fell in love with me and wanted me to marry him, but I came back to England, although I loved him very much. I have often contemplated suicide, but the thought that this would bring distress on others stopped me. How often I have envied somebody killed in an accident or wished I could contract a fatal disease. I can find no comfort or remission, I cannot go on like this. I have not the courage to keep turning away from the affection that is offered.'

When Alice, after this letter, came to see me, at the age of thirty, she appeared a rather small compact person with a face which, though not beautiful, was attractively intelligent. Her temperament was evidently of a kind which must be considered in some degree neurotic, but it was the temperament which goes with a high degree of mental capacity. Alice was adequately fulfilling, sometimes in London, sometimes in Paris, her duties in a Tourist Agency which involved a knowledge of languages as well as skill in dealing with ignorant or stupid travellers. I had little trouble in dispelling the nightmare which had weighed on her so long, and enabling her to see that she had no occasion for the depression of that inferiority complex of which she thought herself the hopeless victim.

It is pleasant to be able to lighten another's burden so easily. Yet even the ease with which it may be done leaves one a little sad. For how often has it been left undone!

Here is a woman, intelligent, of fine and sensitive character, and evidently attractive, who has been subjected for twelve of the best years of her life to the torture of a crushing burden which it only needed a touch to remove. The world is full of inevitable pains and griefs and anxieties, amply sufficient to supply us with all the discipline we may need. It is stupid, when it is not cruel, usually harmful and at best unnecessary, to make possible a torture which cannot even be told. 'If only adults would realise,' Alice exclaims, 'how children want help!' There is no finer task in life than to let a little light and sunshine into those parts of it which have so long been shut up to fester in darkness.

Alice is married now to the excellent Frenchman whose devotion she had so long thought she was unworthy to accept. Her home is in the South of France and she writes as a happy wife and mother.

XVIII

A NEW MOTHER

MARGERY is a devoted correspondent who lives at a secluded spot on the Pacific Coast. I have never seen her, but I have a more intimate knowledge of her than one usually has of even the people who are nearest. She feels that it is possible to say to someone on the other side of the world the things which one would not dare, for that world itself, to say in one's own household. Margery finds a great satisfaction in saying them. She has a rich and varied nature and I am interested in all her aspects. In one of these aspects she is among what I call the 'New Mothers.' I mean by that term, not of course all mothers, but a growing proportion with special features which distinguish them from the mothers of yesterday whose ideal was to indulge children and protect them from the results of that indulgence, and from the mothers of the day before yesterday who inculcated obedience above everything, and sought to mould their children by a discipline imposed from outside.

The New Mother refuses to adopt either strenuous despotism or weak indulgence. She desires to be the confident and councillor of her children; she gives them freedom, but she makes them understand that freedom means responsibility, for she knows that the discipline involved by experience is a far better preparation for life than an artificially imposed discipline. I am reminded of Margery when I think of Alice whose early life might have been so much happier if she had had a 'New Mother' to guide her.

Margery's conception of child-training is the outcome of her own observation and her experience with her own girls of whom the eldest has now reached the age of puberty. She has brought them up from infancy naked, or with a minimum of necessary clothing, accustoming them to a graduated amount of sunshine from the age of eight weeks. They slept out of doors during the daytime, and while feedings were frequent the babies were never waked or urged to feed. They taught themselves to walk, and were given as much freedom as possible, under her own eyes, so that a prohibitive 'No' should seldom be needed. 'Every possible thing that they could do alone,' Margery writes, 'or even half-do, I allowed and encouraged them to do. I've never said: "You can't do this or that"; I've said: "You can try" or "Of course you can do it," or: "By trying you'll learn to do it," and I have helped when asked. When possible, I have let them do what I was doing, "real" things, like cooking, washing, scrubbing, sewing, etc., and let them enjoy the idea that they were helping me, even when the help was questionable.' These children have a voice over their own garments and their own meals, and under such conditions quickly learn to handle objects and co-ordinate their actions. They roller-skate, bicycle, swim, and can handle a boat with confidence and ease, never being forced or taught, the parents simply standing by.

'I have met the subject of death with them,' Margery continues, 'without emotion. It's natural and a part of life. Sex has been faced in the same calm fashion. I never bring the subject up, but I never "shy" when it comes up naturally, and I always answer simply and directly. I feel it most important that their earliest impressions on these matters should come from me, and they are only bored by the chatter of more ignorant children at school.' When they reach the age of seven it is made clear to them that there are such things as duties, that there are small jobs which must be regarded as work and cheerfully borne. School is not enforced. It is considered a privilege; they take pride in their tasks, and each is fully up to standard. They prepare themselves for school in the morning, and if they make mistakes or forget they naturally have to suffer. But they do not go full time to school before the age of ten, and when the school authorities prove troublesome Margery insists that the system must be made to fit the child, and not the child to fit the system. Too much school benumbs the child. This home-life proves so educative that the children are not found backward when at last they go regularly to school, but on the contrary get to the top.

Margery by no means idealises her children. She knows and understands their individual differences; she is able to detect their little weaknesses and vices, is not worried about them, and believes it is usually best to take no notice, for there is often a reason for them. She knows, too, her own weaknesses and imperfections (so do I), and is sometimes willing that her children also should know them; this arouses in them a sympathetic consideration which has not been taught but springs up naturally. It seems clear that a psychoanalyst would derive little nourishment from this family. Obedience has here for the most part given place to responsiveness, and after puberty to co-operation and confidence. The mother who has not attained that result by the time adolescence is reached must be regarded, Margery feels, as a failure.

New Mothers, I said at the outset, are still a minority. They are surrounded by mothers of the old sort who, actively or passively, impede their movements. All the skill and the discretion of the New Mothers are needed to meet that opposition. But the future belongs to them. Alice, like Margery herself, had an Old Mother. But Alice herself is a New Mother. And, with the like early warning, how many more!

I may perhaps add that I showed one of Margery's letters to my friend Dr. Winifred de Kok, who agreed with me as to Margery's claim to be regarded as a 'New Mother,' and has quoted the letter in full at the end of her admirable book *New Babes for Old.*

XIX

THE SIGNIFICANCE OF WAR

My Swedish correspondent is not altogether satisfied with my solution of his difficulty concerning the substitute for war. He fears I have not fully understood his question. He puts it afresh and would be thankful for an answer.

'I understand perfectly the necessity for Death and Pain as essential elements of life. But I ask you, who have thought about it so much more than I have: What shall we put in the place of war so long as the people are what they are nowadays? You see, I lecture much on disarmament as one of our present problems. Humanity's blood-thirst is recognised thoroughly enough. We know what kind of nature we have: uncivilised, primitive, bloodthirsty. Now if people come to me and say they see the idiocy of war and ask what we are to set in its place as an outlet for our primitive blood-thirst, what shall I tell them?'

The half of knowledge, as Bacon so long ago shrewdly remarked, lies in asking the right question. What I have to say to my Swedish friend is that he has not asked the right question. He wishes to know with what we can replace human blood-thirst. I can only reply that there is no such 'blood-thirst' to replace.

Not only is the assumption unjustified that Man is a bloodthirsty animal, it is not truly correct to say that any animals, whether along the line of man's ancestry, or any other related line, not even among the carnivora who are remote from man, are 'bloodthirsty.' What is wrongly called 'blood-thirst' is in animals merely the expression of hunger or jealousy, that is to say it is simply the by-product of the two fundamental and entirely legitimate instincts of nutrition and of sex. They are not seeking to shed blood, they are seeking either food or a mate, and it may truly be said that in most cases they do so with the minimum of bloodshed.

Even the most dreaded and occasionally dangerous animals, such as lions and tigers, are not essentially bloodthirsty, but spend most of their time peacefully. They are capable of affection, even for so hostile a creature as man, and we are told of tigers who, after an absence of many years, remember and show every sign of affection for persons they had formerly known. To strangers they can be harmless. Recently a woman on entering her cottage not far from London stumbled against an escaped tiger and rushed out in horror. Shortly afterwards the tiger, having done no harm beyond accidentally breaking a small vase, emerged from the house and retired contentedly into captivity, feeling, no doubt, after this first visit to a human habitation, that one glimpse of the home-life of mankind is enough. I have not the slightest doubt, however, that an age will come when the lion and the tiger will be domesticated, like the cat, which is related to the tiger, and the dog which is related, however obscurely, to the wolf.

As to Man, the old legend that he practiced war from the beginning is no longer acceptable. Personal squabbles and fights, such as occur in all communities, are not necessarily connected with war. We cannot easily conceive of wars in the Paleolithic Age which lasted for so vast a period of time, and the Eskimo of today, whom some scientists would regard as relics of the races of that early Stone Age, are without war. It was among the settled and organised communities of Neolithic days, and especially in the early metal ages, that conflicts fairly to be called war-like seem first to have appeared. For it was then that property became an important element in life, and property, with all that flows from it, soon became the great motive for war, as indeed, however concealed a motive, it may be said to be still. Other motives came in as so-called civilisation developed, but none of them have their source in blood-thirst; and some of them make an appeal to exalted impulses.

It is unfortunate that Freud, and some other psychoanalysts — who seem sometimes to show a malicious pleasure in trying to give an evil aspect to human impulses — should have regarded hate as a primary motive and love as a secondary derivative. From an evolutionary viewpoint it is not easy to make this work out; the reverse order would be far more plausible. Those crustaceans which carry their hard skeletons outside may be fairly well equipped to survive in a world of hate. But the human animal, so defenceless in early life, with an infancy of such unparalleled length, could not survive unless bathed in a perpetual atmosphere of love. Hate indeed can only be regarded in its origin as a secondary reaction of love. We hate that which threatens what we love. The contempt which is nowadays felt for the old conception of a sentimental universe of love is reasonable enough. But it must not lead us to the opposite and equally absurd conception of a universe of hate. There is love as well as hate, and much that we count hate is often the result of a preventible accident.

Accidents must of course occur in human as in animal society, when there is a lack of proper super-national control. In the London Zoological Gardens two snakes of different but allied species lived together, until lately, and in peaceful amity. One evening last week, four rats were placed in their cage as a meal to be shared. Next morning the keeper found no rats and only one snake, and that enormously swollen. The exact sequence of events in this unfortunate incident can only be surmised. — It must not be too hastily assumed that I have in mind the situation presented by Japan and China and Manchuria.

XX

UTOPIA HERE AND NOW

A CORRESPONDENT, who mischievously suspects me of Utopian tendencies, would like to know how I view the new discovery that Utopias are not only realisable but pernicious when realised.

It is quite true that Aldous Huxley took as a motto for his brilliant and fascinating *Brave New World* a statement to that effect. To a Christianised Bolshevist like Berdyaeff the Five Years Plan was, naturally enough, a milestone on the road of human perdition: 'Utopias appear today much more realisable than was formerly believed. How to avoid Utopia is becoming a question full of anguish.'

But I refuse to admit that the discovery that Utopias may be realised can be regarded as new. Every Utopia seems indeed an impossible dream when it is first put forward, but later, as H. G. Wells has said of More's Utopia, it seems 'very unimaginative.' Some of the features of the world More described may indeed seem to us undesirable, or merely quaint, but to a considerable extent we are all living now in More's Utopia. We have the Utopian religious tolerance, at all events to the extent that we burn neither Catholics nor Protestants; we are approaching the Utopian six hours day, with leisure for all and education for all; we have in an increasing degree the Utopian divorce by mutual consent; we have long regarded as commonplace the Utopian method of incubating eggs by artificial heat.

But Sir Thomas More was executed. A later Utopian,

Thomas Paine, only escaped the same fate by an accident at the last moment, and would have been killed many times over if the vituperation which has assailed him until almost our own time could have been translated into action. Even his 'beloved America,' as he called the Republic he had helped to establish, would have done little for his memory if it were not for the literary monument erected to him by an anglicised American of distinction, Moncure Conway. I seek in vain through the East Anglian town which had the honour to give him birth for any memorial to its most famous son. Yet, although we have not so far reached the 'Republic of Europe' he foretold, the political and social world — even to some extent the material world for he possessed engineering insight — in which we now live is run largely on the lines laid down by that Prince of Utopians who seemed to so many of his contemporaries really too mad or too wicked to be kept alive. For nothing is so dangerous in the world of today as to foresee the world of tomorrow.

But it is not merely in modern times that we live in Utopia. We have never lived anywhere else. We may have different theories about the mechanism of life but it is certainly possible to regard it as from the first an inspiring endeavour — what the psychologist might call a conation — towards an unconscious when not conscious end which at the moment before it began to take shape was strictly Utopian. Even the story of creation in the book of Genesis is merely the narrative of the establishment in the Divine Mind of an Utopian Universe out of chaos. When we come to our anthropoid ancestors, descending from their tree tops to generate that strangest of Utopian creatures called Man, we reach a climax in this process, and those who only now begin to view the realisation of Utopias with alarm may be a million years too late.

If it is true, as we are warned, that the time is coming when the realisation of Utopia will prove a source of anguish, that will merely prove that we have built Utopia badly. Even then the freer and less 'perfect' world we shall thus be led to seek will only be another Utopia.

XXI

ROUSSEAU

Nᴏᴛ having the pleasure of being known to you, it will no doubt seem strange that I should take the step of writing to you; perhaps even I shall appear ridiculous when at my first words you will understand the object of my letter. But why should I be afraid? You know the human heart too well not to know all its agitations. Mine needs to be opened, and entirely, but it can only do so to you. In you alone I feel trust, for you are the only person whose arguments convince and help me.'

No! these words were not addressed to me. This time I am quoting from a long letter — the burden of which is 'Teach me to live' — written nearly a century before I was born, on the 26th of March, 1764. It was written by a woman living in Paris who simply signed herself 'Henriette' and was addressed to Rousseau.

Without seeking or desiring it, he received a vast number of such letters from strangers, but he accepted them seriously and often answered them in the spirit in which they were written. At one time he even planned to publish a volume of them. They came from men and women, people of various kinds and classes. Even a young Protestant pastor wrote: 'My dear Master, I will seek to follow in the footsteps of Jesus Christ and yours.' Henriette's letter is by no means the earliest, but we happen to have it in full, with Rousseau's answer, and it is evidently typical.

Today, no doubt, there are not a few writers who receive

such letters from persons they have never seen. I could certainly bring forward counterparts from my own correspondence. But it is interesting to go back to the period when they began and to the man who first received them. That the man was Rousseau I have little doubt. Great teachers had devoted disciples long before Rousseau. We have but to read the Bible. They have flocked to every teacher who seemed able to convey the message of life. But the relationship was always a personal one, of contact in time and place, and even when epistolary, as again we see in the Bible by the letters of St. Paul, it was with groups or individuals already known personally.

It was a part of the great revolution effected in our world by Rousseau — a totally undesigned part — that he introduced a new means of spiritual communication. It was a scarcely less notable innovation for his time than the radio communication in ours, and of a similar nature. That is to say it enabled anyone to come into touch at a distance with what seemed a radiant centre of light and power.

Therein the peculiar potency of Rousseau's genius was manifested. He was the most spiritually naked person who had appeared in our civilisation. Such nakedness had never before been accompanied by so sensitive a humanity, so many weaknesses, so serious and sincere an aspiration towards an ultimate purification, and so complete a self-absorption. It was a self urgent for immediate satisfaction, not content, like the idle world around, to postpone Paradise to a future life, but demanding salvation, and for all, here and now. Yet all that might have counted for nothing if this man had not chanced to be a supreme artist who found his material in that all-absorbing self. He created the French language anew; he gave it the power to embody the most intimate sighs of the heart (has not a great mystic said that God is an unutterable sigh?), so that they could be borne afar to penetrate innumerable kindred hearts. Some of his eloquence has, through its very success, become dull to our ears, yet always enough remains to bear witness to the achievement. For in everything he was himself, his genuine self. It amuses me to remember that he wrote even the lists of his dirty linen for the laundress with as careful and elegant calligraphy as his love-letters, and preserved them — where they may still be seen — among his most important papers. It was characteristic. It is a trait of that genius which makes Rousseau unique.

There have always been estimable academic people in circles who have counted it a solemn duty to demolish, or at all events to vituperate, Rousseau. For almost everything evil in our world today Rousseau has been regarded as the source. There is no consistency in Rousseau's doctrines, and it is an easy task to expose their falsity; he may indeed be said to have done it first of all himself. Yet, when it is done, all that is essential in Rousseau remains intact. He has still been the inspiration not merely of all our political Republics but of our great philosophical guides and artistic creators from Kant to Tolstoy. There is something more in life than the beautifully rational systems which alone appeal to our professors, and books about Rousseau are still pouring every year from the press, while the complete edition of his letters — the greatest of those Confessions of which his whole life consisted — is only now appearing in some twenty splendidly edited volumes.

To heave half a brick at Rousseau will no doubt continue

to remain a favourite athletic exercise of our professors. We need not fear that it will harm anyone; on the contrary it can only do good. There are many things we need that are not to be found in Rousseau, nor can it be claimed — he was himself the first to disclaim it — that he was an object for admiration. How few of us are! Yet it still remains true that the spiritual atmosphere of our modern world — such as it is! — reached us from Rousseau.

XXII

WHAT IS A RADICAL?

I HAVE lately had a difference of opinion with an esteemed correspondent, active and distinguished in various fields among the more advanced writers of America today. As a rule we succeed in maintaining a harmonious relationship, and the present misunderstanding arose out of the different meanings which we attach to the same word. The bone of contention over which, quite politely and considerately, we snarled at each other, was the word 'Radical.'

It appears to be rather an alarming word in America today, but my correspondent bravely assumes it for himself, since in his ideology there are only two groups of social thinkers today, the Reactionaries and the Radicals. The particular figure whose name had come into our correspondence in this connection was Professor Westermarck, the well-known historian of marriage. My friend dismissed him as a Reactionary; from my English viewpoint Westermarck, whether for good or evil, might better be called a Radical, and certainly not a Reactionary, even though he might re-act against what my correspondent called Radicalism.

I was assuming for the word Radical the sense which it has always worn in England where it originated. Radicalism flourished vigorously in the middle of the nineteenth century. In politics it was democratic, in social philosophy it was individualistic, in religion it was rationalist. Towards the State Radicalism was grudging, if not hostile; social progress seemed to lie in throwing off the old fetters of the State, and resisting any new encroachments. Free trade, Trades-Unionism, co-operation, all forms of individualistic self-help, were largely inspired by Radicals.

In my youth I came slightly in contact with some of the old Radical leaders although I was of too young a generation to be close to them. That indeed was the moment in England when Radicalism, having largely fulfilled its mission — though it is still carried on more quietly today — fell into the background as a new and different wave, which we termed Socialism then and today Communism, broke violently on our shores. Many of the old Radicals regarded this new movement as reactionary; it seemed a fresh manifestation, even if in a Revolutionary form, of that effete statism and that bureaucratic domination which they had spent their lives in combating. Had anyone suggested to them that Karl Marx and the other initiators of the new movement were 'Radicals' they would have repelled the insinuation with all the energy they could command.

But for my friend in New York it is precisely Karl Marx who is the great Radical champion. Therewith the clash between his American system of values and mine based on English traditions. Each of us brought forward his own conception of the Radical and each assumed that the other accepted it. But we were assuming the likeness of two things of the same name which were not only different but even opposed.

My friend and I speedily understood this point and we have wisely arranged that the difference is to be cleared up when we meet and can discuss it, for it is useless to talk in terms which constantly move further and further away from the point to which they should converge. 'Of course,'

he writes, 'you are perfectly right about the use of the word
"radical." It is so loose that the word itself is almost useless.
The thing I am driving at is concerned with a society that
is non-individualistic but collectivistic, and in such a society
concepts that were tenable in an individualistic society
become outmoded and more or less worthless. On reaching
England I shall naturally see you, and at such a time we can
discuss these points, I hope, at considerable length.'

I bring this little discussion forward here not because I am
greatly concerned with the label to affix to Westermarck or
even with the connotation of the word Radical, but because
I am profoundly convinced of the importance of what has
lately been emphasised as *definitional clarity*. The fiercest
battles between men have often had their origin in the meaning of words. In the early ages of Christianity thousands
were eternally damned and even temporally destroyed over
disputes having their origin in subtle theological shades of
meaning which to the unsympathetic observer have seemed
a conflict of Tweedledum and Tweedledee. Even if now less
acute in the theological field, bloodthirsty quarrels of the
same character still arise. What, for instance, at the present
day is meant by the word 'Security'? Why must one nation
threaten to fly at the throats of other nations which do not
accept its conception of the meaning of that word?

Disputes of a less tragic but still significant sort are specially
apt to arise, as my correspondent and I have found, through
the common use of English on two sides of the Ocean. We
cannot too carefully examine the use of words we inherit
when they have developed in two separate lands along two
different lines of tradition. Whatever else we do or leave
undone, let us concentrate on definitional clarity.

XXIII

THE RELIGION OF BOLSHEVISM

I AM assuming the privilege of presenting to you an Idea,'
writes from California a correspondent who encloses
various documents. 'I am expecting to know whether
I shall come forth as a teacher of the doctrine of Integration,
the validity of which I clearly realise. But before we can
proceed to Integrate, that is to say to make Whole, a pair of
limits must be established. Now it is a recent discovery that
one of these was definitely established by Buddha as representing the Scientific Outlook, and the other by Christ as
representing the Mystical Outlook. Upon the basis of this
great religious discovery I believe we are entering the Age
of Integration. But can we enter it unhindered by tradition?
Must not those who stand for the Scientific Outlook and
those who stand for the Mystical Outlook first learn more
about each other? What is your estimate of the situation?'

It will probably be guessed that the estimate was not forth-
coming. But I should like to explain here exactly why I have
submitted no estimate. It is by no means because I take
lightly my correspondent's problem. On the contrary, I
consider that he has gone to the heart of what is for many
people the most fundamental difficulty they have to grapple
with: how to reconcile the claims of science and of religion.
That is to say how to have at the same time both what they
can regard as a truthful picture of the universe and the
peace of a home-feeling in that universe which passes all
understanding. That reconciliation is for many the key to

fruitful activity and abiding happiness in the world. But it is a key the individual must find for himself. Having found it, having discovered that it opens the door, he needs no assurance of its validity. He possesses faith, which means essentially not, as is sometimes supposed, a belief in a delusion—though it easily may be merely that—but an actually experienced assurance embodied in the individual's total outlook. When this is present no assurance is needed from outside.

If my estimate of the situation means anything, then my correspondent's doctrine of Integration may seem nothing in the world. As a matter of fact, it seems to me to represent a way of coming near to the problem, though its phraseology and its formulas are peculiar. But I remain of the opinion that no outsider can here intrude, whether to offer a solution or to criticise. It is, as they phrased it of old time, a matter between a man and his Maker.

At the same time I fully admit that the question of religion has a wider bearing. It so happens that this wider bearing is of recent years brought very vividly before us. Today, for the first time in two thousand years, we may see religion on the old mass-production scale at work in the world as it never has been since Christianity was young.

Many observers are puzzled to account for the immense interest felt by the young of various lands in the Soviet doings in Russia. It has been attributed to the warm welcome offered by the Bolshevists, to the youthful interest in empirical experimentation, to the fascination of crusading, and so on. But the real fascination behind these surfaces lies in the fact that it is a religion, a real religion, not a mere creed such as our own Churches are wont to profess and therewith rest content. The religion of Communism is no mere economic theory; it is a motive force which lifts the individual out of himself and makes him glad to take part in the reconstruction of the world on a new foundation. It subjects the individual to a great super-individual end. It brings back the conception of life as service. That is the conception that ruled when Christianity was a vast motive force in the world. Just as the Christians gladly endured torture and death, or faced the lions in the amphitheatre, so the Communists are indifferent to hunger and fatigue, always upheld by the vision of a future Heaven upon earth.

No one has of late brought this out more clearly than Nicholas Berdyaeff. He sees Communism as a religion striving to take the place of Christianity, and his horror of Communism is intensified by the fact that he is himself a Russian, once Professor of Philosophy at Moscow under the Soviet until he was exiled nearly ten years ago. And the significant thing about his hatred of Communism is that he seems to realise that its methods are those by which Christianity conquered the world two thousand years ago. There is almost a poignant despair in his tone when he asks if Christianity is now bankrupt.

It must seem to many a question easier to ask than to answer. Christianity in the old world, like Communism in Russia today, arose among peoples to whom spiritual mass-production was still easy to achieve, and a standardised religion a natural ideal. How far is that possible for the civilised Westerner of today? Are we, as Berdyaeff desires and Gerald Heard expects, to look for a new religious collectivism on the old Christianised basis? Or, as I can myself alone find possible, to embrace the adventure of a spiritual individualism?

XXIV

THE DIFFICULTY OF POLITICS

As an admirer of your philosophy and work,' writes a woman of distinguished intelligence whom I will here call Frances, 'I would like to ask you a question which has puzzled me of late: What attitude can a decent mortal adopt towards politics at large and the government of his own country in particular? As to most activities of life I seem to be endowed not only with enough power of æsthetic contemplation to be an interested spectator, but with enough vigorous activity to be, here and there, on a small scale, a willing participator. But in the sphere of politics I have to content myself with being an intellectual anarchist. This whole field of human affairs seems to embody Man's lowest impulses, where only disappointment awaits the person of fine ideals who endeavours to take a part, though one often attempts it in youth. No matter what the form of government, it seems never to secure more than crude and rough management of affairs, with such results as poverty, wholesale miseries, and catastrophes like the last Great War. I have come to look upon it as a grim joke of Fate; though I take an active share in life on other sides, in the hope that men of good will may perhaps some day bring us nearer to that æsthetic revolution you speak of in *The Dance of Life*. I am now nearing fifty; I have, like so many others, suffered to the full the horrors of the War; but now, seeing that chaos and misery which have always prevailed among human beings have in our time been heightened by our rulers, I come to ask: Is Man always doomed to be crushed by his politicians and governments?'

I can honestly tell my friend that I am much in sympathy with her attitude. But I would remind her that in the book she mentions, where all human operations are regarded as of the nature of art, it is pointed out how endlessly difficult are those arts of which the material is human beings. It is hard enough to be an artist when the material is lifeless and unconscious matter with no resisting will of its own. But new difficulties begin at once and never cease when the material is alive and possessed of aims which may be opposed to those of the artist and even to its own best interests. Difficulties may come in even when there are only two persons, and they are both seeking the same end; whence it is the art of love is still so rare.

The home, again, is a small state which ought to be incomparably easier to rule than a nation. A general unity of interests and harmonious working are here so obviously needed and apparently so easily within reach. Yet Frances, who among her other aptitudes is a skilful housewife, well knows how seldom they are attained, even when on the surface there is a pretence of attainment. Husband and wife have to be adjusted to each other, children to their parents and to each other, and there are as well endless little problems of domestic service without which everything goes wrong. So rare is the good government of the home that the whole institution is constantly being attacked (ask Dr. Schmalhausen!) and there are some who would abolish the family altogether.

A nation is infinitely more difficult to organise than a domestic home. Indeed, when I contemplate the attacks on the home and the pleas for the abolition of the family, I wonder we are not oftener asked to abolish nations. There must surely be many good reasons for running the world smoothly and peacefully on non-national lines. A new field of activity seems here to be open for those who are opposed to any League of Nations.

Meanwhile, however, we can only deal with the problem as it exists. I hope one may be excused for making the obvious remark that, exceedingly difficult as that problem remains, the solution is always in our own hands. It is a long time since Jefferson wrote to John Adams: 'I agree with you that there is a natural aristocracy among men. The grounds of this are virtue and talents. The natural aristocracy I regard as the most precious gift of Nature for the instruction, the trusts and governments of society. May we not even say that that form of government is the best which provides the most effectually for a pure selection of these *aristoi* into the offices of Government?' They are wise words, and the sting of them is in the tail, in the stress on *selection*, which is impossible without instruction, education in the widest sense, to which Jefferson himself devoted so much of his fine energies, and which yet so often fills us with despair.

'Every society has the criminals it deserves,' declared a great French criminologist of the last century. A society does not indeed select its criminals; still it produces them, they are a by-product of its own intimate activities. But a society not only produces its politicians; by its votes it selects them. There can be no escape from the conclusion: Every society has the politicians it deserves.

XXV

GEORGE SAND

BETTY, who is now less occupied in tending her baby, has become interested in George Sand, and writes to ask me what books of hers I should recommend.

That question, like many others, is easier to ask than to answer. It is so for me, since it happens that I regard George Sand as one of the great figures of the modern world and yet, although she was writing copiously throughout a long life, I do not consider her to be the author of any supremely great book. To that extent I might seem to be in agreement with the contemptuous disparagement with which for many years her name has been met, especially in her own land of France. Yet for me she remains great, alike in her pioneering personality, in her attitude towards life, and even in the exuberant stream of her unceasing literary activity.

There is a special reason, apart from Betty's question, for speaking of her now. This year is the centenary of the publication of *Indiana*, one of her earlier novels and not the best, but that which created the greatest sensation and no doubt served as the foundation of her fame. Like so many of her later books, it came from the heart (whence many artists think that books ought not to come) and was rooted in personal experience. Aurore, Baroness Dudevant, as she then was, may be said to have been born with a predisposition for daring personal experiences and in an environment to favour their expansion. On the paternal side she was remotely of royal descent through her great grandfather

Maurice de Saxe, great adventurer, soldier, lover, and artist, while her mother was a proletarian, at best a little dress-maker, a characteristic product of Parisian streets, totally unable to understand her wonderful daughter. The young girl was married in her teens to a commonplace youth of aristocratic family and low tastes who never made love to her, and was so dense that he considered his wife stupid. A separation took place after children had been born. Then George Sand, at the age of twenty-six, went to Paris, just after the Revolution of 1830, when the air was charged with electric energy, entered into all its life, began to know the meaning of love, and set to work to earn her living by her pen.

The Indiana-Aurore of the novel is married to an excellent man who is devoted to her and allows her extraordinary freedom. There is really nothing wrong with him, except for the one great defect that she does not love him. She becomes attracted to a man who may be considered the conventional Frenchman of gallantry, gay and brilliant; she offers to go away with him; he repulses her. All the time there is close beside her an English cousin Ralph, the typical Englishman of fiction, phlegmatic, silent, tenderly sentimental, devoted to Indiana, though he never tells his love, and always at hand in moments of danger. At last she divines his devotion and responds to it. Finally, after her husband is dead, they leave France to seek suicide together in the most romantically beautiful spot they can find.

Whatever we may now think of the story so deeply marked by the French Romantic movement which it helped to create, George Sand had poured into it the passionate revolt of her own life at the moment, and she had the genius to make her characters vividly alive. Moreover, here was virtually a new situation in fiction. Madame de Staël had a few years earlier claimed freedom in her novels for the woman of genius; and it was a rather invidious and pretentious claim to make. George Sand made the claim for any woman, as the simple outcome of her human and social position. That was a more revolutionary demand and we can understand its far-reaching echoes. It is sometimes said, not altogether without truth, that they came down to Ibsen and have inspired women's movements that are only now really influential in the world.

Yet it is characteristic of George Sand's many-sided and exuberant nature that she was no doctrinaire preacher of women's rights, and not even in reality the advocate of free-love. At a volcanic moment this woman could pour out the burning lava of *Indiana*, yet in later life she could be described by unsympathetic observers as cow-like, and could sincerely glorify faithful monogamy. She was domesticated, maternal even in love, so devoted to a peaceful country existence that perhaps her most nearly perfect books are those that depict rural life. It is part of the distinction of George Sand that she was entirely woman, with nothing man-like about her; the name and the occasional adoption at one time of masculine dress being simply for social convenience. It is also a part, a more remarkable part, of that distinction that she was accepted, almost from the first. Every path was opened to her; she quickly became one of the most popular writers of her time; all the great literary figures and artists of the day, from Balzac down, were proud to treat her with affection and regard as a comrade, while abroad she could win the enthusiastic admiration of so respectable a Victorian (even if a rebel at heart) as Mrs. Browning.

In old age her correspondence with Flaubert constitutes a fascinating memorial. No two people could be more unlike, she who had lived so freely on every side, he who had been a cloistered monk of art, and poured as much contempt on the world for which she had worked and suffered as any monk of old. Their opinions often differed, and it is amusing to observe that it is the woman who had drunk deeply of the bitter cup of life, and experienced so many delusions, who has grown wise and serene, not the fierce ascetic who had despised life. But no differences ever disturbed their tender friendship.

'I have been called a modern George Sand ("but so much better looking, my dear") but I have never gone about making a sort of slogan of it.' So I read in the confessions of an admired young literary woman of today. She was wise not to make a sort of slogan of it, and might have been wiser still not to mention it. We esteem those women of our time who have followed where a great-souled pioneer led, but we may leave it to an Elizabeth Browning to acclaim the George Sand of our time.

XXVI

WHAT IS THE WORTH OF EDUCATION?

AN unknown Indian correspondent, who tells me he is an M.A. and Professor in a college, writes to ask a string of questions. Such as: Are you a non-believer in every religion? What do you think of Lord Jesus Christ? Do you believe there are men now of practical courage equal to Socrates, and pioneers of thought equal to Aristotle and Newton? Do you believe that 'Half knowledge is a dangerous thing.'

I do not know what my readers' reactions may be to such questions. Mine is one of sadness. Not because I am for the most part no better able than anyone else to answer them. It makes me sad that anyone should ask them, or even desire any answer save his own. If on such matters of faith and belief a man cannot form his own opinions and stick to them, in complete indifference to the opinions of other people, what is his opinion worth? What indeed is he himself worth?

There is certainly one question my correspondent asks on which I might comment, the last. What about: 'Half knowledge is a dangerous thing'? Therein he seems to touch the malady I detect in his own soul.

This whole series of questions, in fact, might come from someone — whether or not it actually does — who is suffering from 'half knowledge.' One pictures a student who has been dragged painfully over the surface of the conventional education in school and college of our Western civilization, and retained from it a number of names, a number of vague notions, a number of oft-repeated maxims. But they remain on the student's mental surface, a mere matter for idle enquiries; they have never sunk deep to become entwined in the mental texture, to help to constitute a distinct intellectual and spiritual personality. It makes one sad because one feels that it has everywhere happened all over India. No doubt it was a noble ideal to bring European methods of intellectual training to India and to lay the fruits of our traditions at the feet of an alien race. The European traditions may be all right — though even about that one may sometimes have one's doubts — for us who have our ancestral roots in Europe, but it seems unreasonable to expect them to be right for a people of another colour, of a totally different clime, a different hereditary endowment, who have grown into a social and religious structure as unlike ours as possible. That is a question the Indians themselves are now beginning to ask. And perhaps too late.

But it is not only in India, it is not only among people of a differently tinted skin and soul, that this problem comes before us. Is the education now given in our European and American schools and colleges any less superficial? I cannot find that it is, though the character of it is less obtrusive. That merely means that it is taken less seriously and is still more easily washed off. I can conceive of an education, based on the actual hereditary endowment of the child and rooted in the living environment from which he springs, that would be genuinely interwoven and livingly embodied in the whole texture of his mental nature. That indeed is what took place with the craftsmen who are now dying out. They were early apprenticed to some craft, such as their family had exercised and they were familiar with; they slowly absorbed its principles and acquired the skill to exercise it independently. They became master crafts-men and, if they had it in them, they could rise to the higher intellectual plane of art; many great artists have arisen from the class of craftsmen. The men who have been thus trained show a finer temper in all the affairs of life, and since they know what it is to acquire mastery they are con-siderate of those who have acquired mastery in other than their fields.

Our systems tend to work out in the reverse direction. It is true that in mechanics, in engineering, in electricity, the old craftsman is appearing among us again in a new shape. But for a large part our education is still not a training, nor is it based on the foundation of the individuality to which it is to be applied. We offer no technic which when the pupil has absorbed it will not only make him a master in his own department but also confer on him a wise regard for every technic of life. We only plunge him in a mass of miscellane-ous notions and unimportant facts which cannot form an organised whole or constitute a coherent discipline in which the individual organism has free and independent play. Not only are they all speedily forgotten, but they engender that supercilious attitude of mind among us which dismisses all genuine technic and discipline of the soul with superior contempt.

I have referred to the hereditary foundation as an essential part of the problem of education. That means that when you plant the seeds of education you must know beforehand what soil, if any, there is to feed those seeds. Strange as it may seem, it is only of recent years that this fundamental question has been investigated by the skilled examination of brains, and not merely by the more obvious tests of cranial capacity, not individually reliable. Of late this has specially been done by Gordon and Vint in Nairobi, on East African natives, among whom are striking differences in various tribes and low degrees of mentality among some. The microscopic relationships of the parts of the brain cortex held to be the physical basis of mind, compared to those that are the physical seat of the animal impulses vary, and show as compared with Europeans, six per cent more physical basis, while the Europeans show over nine per cent more basis of mind. It is fruitless and perhaps disastrous to apply to these Africans European methods of education, and among Europeans, as we are beginning to see, we cannot apply to the backward and defective the methods which, more or less badly, we apply to the normal. Our seed, even if good seed, is sown in vain on the dry sand or the hard rock.

It is not my wish to criticise teachers. I have been one myself, and can sympathise with their difficulties. They know the futility of systems set up by ignorant and prejudiced politicians. But for the most part they are helpless, galley-slaves chained to oars they have not themselves made.

That is why I would sometimes like to see thrown aside all this burden of education and a new beginning made.

XXVII

DO WOMEN RESEMBLE MEN?

A WOMAN doctor has sent me a big book in which she expounds what she conceives to be the proper place of woman in the world. She seems to feel assured that I shall be in agreement with her, as indeed I altogether am when she asserts that a woman should not try to be a bad imitation of a man, but rather to be an equal who is independently co-operative. That seems very much the sort of doctrine which I have always been trying to make clear. So I am rather shocked to find that at the very outset of her book my correspondent asserts that the physiological differences between the two sexes are slight and the psychological differences have no natural existence at all, being entirely artificial.

This calm statement shocks me because I happen long ago to have published a big book, *Man and Woman*, based on the collective and careful sifting during many years of the related scientific data demonstrating as clearly as possible by measurable relationships not only that 'taken on the average a man is a man even to his thumbs and a woman is a woman down to her little toes,' but much more than that. As had long been suspected, and is now growing clearer day by day, our psychological characteristics are closely associated with the physiological activities of the endocrine gland system. By the varying endocrine characteristics one individual differs from another individual, and notably one sex differs from the other sex. Even so far as each sex possesses the same glands they differ in energy and balance. A woman is a woman, it has been said by a distinguished authority, by virtue of the totality of her internal secretions. The equality, or rather the equivalence, of the sexes is becoming generally recognised. But, as the late Professor Manouvrier, an advocate of the rights of women, pointed out, such equivalence does not mean resemblance.

One would have thought that by today this fundamental truth would have become a truism, and that a woman, especially a woman physician, would have been the last to deny it. For not only is it a demonstrable fact, but if it were not so the situation would be rather deplorable. If women are merely for the most part slightly smaller men — men with less power and less range of activity — then the result of giving them an equal place in life with men is simply to weaken the total force of the human race. The reason why we believe that in placing women side by side with men we enrich and strengthen the race is precisely because they are different. And in maintaining that complementary relationship we are true to the relationship of male and female in Nature generally.

As I write in the garden this spring day, a wren on a low branch close by is singing continuously his loud sweet song. The wren, though a very small bird, has always been accorded a certain importance (in French folklore even as 'little king') and, after the robin, he is the least shy of our English birds. So he is not dismayed by my near presence. After a time one may observe what is going on. His mate is building the nest on the ground below. She appears bearing a wisp of straw, and disappears in the nest for some time, for the wren is a peculiarly careful builder and demands a high degree of finish in the family home. Then she emerges and rests for a few moments on a branch not far from her mate, who continues singing while she proceeds with her operations by bringing further material.

Here we have what seems an unusual sexual distribution of activities. To some persons, indeed, it may seem the familiar case of domestic work for the female and indolence for the male. But if the attitude of the couple were put into conscious thought it might well be that each partner would regard its own activity as essential to the task. Each is exerting much the same amount of energy. Each demands the other's energy, and if the male were absent the nest would not be built.

The wren does not present the sole sexual pattern of life in Nature. There are many patterns. But nearly everywhere the male's part is different from the female's. So far from such difference having no natural foundation and being entirely artificial, we may say exactly the opposite. Let us emphasise the natural equivalence of women with men in any well-constituted society. Let us also recognise their difference.

XXVIII

THE INSULARITY OF THE FRENCH

AN old friend, an artist and a lover of France, which he knows well, writes to me on returning to that land that he is more than ever impressed by the insularity of the French. I am struck by this remark, not only because it is not the obvious thing to say, but because it happens to be a remark I have of late sometimes made to myself. I hasten to add that my friend is not speaking in disparagement, for he has a delicate appreciation of the fine qualities of the French mind. He realises that, more than any other people, the French, on the foundation of a long and unbroken tradition, have built up a great style of life, in every department of which they are fine artists.

Insularity being the quality of living in an island, and Britain being the most conspicuous country of the West confined within islands, we conventionally regard the English as insular. But there is a physical insularity and a spiritual insularity, and they have no necessary connection. The sea in our time is not an insulating medium; it is on the contrary an admirable method of communication with the world. The British have often been insular in social manners (though even that is scarcely true of the peoples of Scotland and Ireland and Wales), but they have shown a great aptitude for living and flourishing outside their islands, and this is true not only of the ordinary population, but of their most distinguished men. In a study of British genius which I made many years ago I found that throughout the course of English history a large proportion of the most eminent men, even when we exclude soldiers, sailors, and explorers, spent abroad considerable parts of their lives, varying from one year to forty years; that was true even for the earliest figure in my list, St. Patrick.

Nothing of the kind could be said of France, except in some degree at special moments, as in the days of Louis XIV when there was a wave of French migration across the world. Even the African colonisation of the last century was due to the initiative of one or two politicians and was at first against the French grain, while the international French restlessness since the Great War is confined to the small circle of intelligentsia, who formerly spent their lives on the Parisian boulevards, but now prefer to be found on the Congo or in Siam or even New York. The main French population are unchanged.

It chances that this same opinion of the French has lately been expressed by a distinguished German critic, Ernst Robert Curtius, who in addition to deep knowledge shows great admiration and affection for France. At the same time he insists on that quality of self-absorption, which I term insularity, as marking the French mind to a peculiar degree. It takes various shapes: in a serious personification as 'La France'; in an exaltation of the country as a perfectly formed land combining all good qualities without excess or extremes; and in a corresponding consciousness of the superiority of the French mind. The result is a certain insularity. That is to say there is an inability to understand the individuality of other nations, or to accept their inevitable reaction to this insularity.

It is to be noted that this criticism comes from a German

indeed, but a lover of France. It is not a condemnation.
Nor is it forgotten that France is not always marked by insular self-absorption, though that attitude seems to predomi-
nate in recent French governments. Mrs. Browning was not
altogether talking nonsense when she referred to France as
that 'poet among the nations.' There are many persons,
who, after (some would say before) their own country, prefer to live in France.

In old days insularity represented a blameless national
sentiment and a workable national policy. It has ceased to
do so today. The countries of the world are slowly — of late
almost rapidly — becoming a single unit. They are even
becoming an economic unity. Production and consumption,
we see, when left to chance lead to disaster. The country
which produces at random, without regard to the necessities
of other countries, is beginning to be seen, not only as the
enemy of human society, but as the agent of its own destruction. The old question: 'Am I my brother's keeper?' is seen
today in a new light when asked by one nation of another,
and is receiving a new answer. A nation no longer lives to
itself or dies to itself. The ancient ideal of national economics
symbolised by the two old ladies who shut their front doors
and lived by taking in each other's washing is out of date,
difficult as it seems for many people to understand this. Are
they at last beginning to understand it in France?

XXIX

THE PLACE OF POLITICIANS

RANCES is not pleased with my attempt to deal with her troubles over politics and politicians. 'I am afraid you do not convince me,' she writes. 'It may be very true that every society has the politicians it deserves. But this is just my trouble! It seems to me that the average intelligence and ability of any society is (and most likely always will be) so low that it never deserves good politicians. When and whence, therefore, can we expect any æsthetic revolution to bring Beauty to guide the affairs of mankind? Again, Jefferson's idea of selection sounds grand. But every form of government has been selected: aristocracy of birth or talent, oligarchy, democracy, Fascist dictators like Mussolini and Communist dictators like Stalin. And under all of them humanity suffers much the same ills and miseries. You talk of our votes. Yet did I not once hear you say at election time: "What is the good of voting? My man always comes at the bottom of the poll!" And you did not vote. Are you not, like me, a non-participator, an intellectual anarchist in this field, because you know it never works, never can?'

I fear that Frances knows too much, and I cannot deny my sympathy with her attitude. Yet I do not retract the principle. We may realise better than the old eighteenth-century men the human weaknesses that remain the same under all governments and the ever-shifting nature of circumstances that can never be calculated beforehand. Of that we are always receiving demonstrations. Even as I write the electors of France are discovering with disgust that the votes they have only just cast are not likely to produce the results they intended; they voted, as they thought, for a leader of the Left, and they find that, wafted by their votes, he is already drifting to the Right.

Yet, even if we never precisely hit the mark, it is surely best to aim at it. We are at all events likely to do better than if we never aim at all. Even at the worst, by strenuously aiming as truly as we know, we have saved our own souls. Our wholesome scepticism, it has always seemed to me, must ever be accompanied by a wholesome optimism. It still remains a pleasure to me to remember that in my first book I wrote that one must set one's shoulder joyously to the world's wheel even though, beforehand, one has slipped that gospel of scepticism, the book of *Ecclesiastes,* underneath one's arm.

There is another consideration I would like here to bring forward, and one, it seems to me, which is really within one's own control. Why, even when admitting the necessity of politicians, should we profess an absurdly impossible idea of their importance? 'The word "politician," ' I read in the May *Forum,* 'calls to mind a man who is slick, pretentious, rather cowardly, and generally intellectually dishonest.' That definition seems put forward to represent the accepted notion; it may not correspond to the superior type. But even when the superior type comes before us, we do all we can to degrade him. We demand of him the impossible and we overwhelm him with insults because he cannot achieve the impossible. The electors who put up a President as the symbol of their favourite ideal — Prosperity or whatever else it may be — and then fall upon him because he cannot achieve what no one could achieve make fools of him and of themselves. They have done their best to bring him down into exactly the shape described by the *Forum's* historian, the shape, that is, of a public man of whom more is expected than any man can possibly accomplish.

Here, indeed, I again join hands with my friend Frances. In this same letter she asks: 'Are not politicians in public life just what the cook or the maidservant is in domestic life? Often indispensable, yet only servants. In the long run, will they not fall into line, just as servants have to lend an ear to their bosses, if only to save their own skins?'

Yes, but we still have to remember that the good servant who 'falls into line' is the servant of the good master. It is ever the intelligence and consideration of the master that makes the good servant. So I end, not by withdrawing from my position, but by strengthening it. If we want sound politics we must learn to know what politics can and cannot achieve, and not put burdens on our politicians which, in the nature of things, they cannot carry. We give them the power to do mischief.

XXX

SEX ENLIGHTENMENT IN EDUCATION

I HAVE been asked to state what I consider to be the place of sexual enlightenment in education and to whom it should be entrusted. Should it be carried on in the school or left to the discretion of the parents?

That is a question which, in one form or another, I have often been asked. I have not always given exactly the same answer, not that my opinions have greatly changed but because it is a subject with such various aspects.

I hold that a course of elementary biological science is an essential part of any school education, and that such a course naturally includes the general facts of sex. But it is clear to me that intimate and personal guidance — it cannot be more than guidance — is the proper business of the parents, above all of the mother, and begins at the earliest age at which a child is able to ask questions. Sex, as we hardly need the psychoanalysts to tell us, has its beginnings in infancy. Moreover, the power of observation begins as early. Today, even the children of decent and superior parents often live under crowded housing conditions which bring the very young child face to face with every sort of experience, good or bad, as soon as its mind is open to any impressions at all. To these the infant mind may respond as it will. To leave it without guidance until the age when school authorities choose to think — and more often choose not to think — that the age has come for sexual knowledge to be imparted, is to be wilfully ignorant and blind before the plain facts of life.

Here what I call the New Mother comes in with her quiet and unobtrusive influence at the outset. There are still far too few such mothers, the friends and trusted counsellors of their children; but how successful they are those who know them may easily find out.

There is additional reason why the mother — that is, the New Mother — should here be the guide. In the production of her child she has been at the heart of sex, and she is not likely to encourage the academic notions which belittle sex and exalt the intellectual aims repressing it. In his finely suggestive book on *Modern Education*, which does much to clarify these questions, Dr. Otto Rank emphasises the need to encourage the ancient belief in the sacredness of sex as the last emotional resource which the exaggerated rationalism of our education has left us.

Does that mean sweeping away our systems of education? Among uncivilised peoples the educational systems seem to be admirable when they consist, as they often do, in a comprehensive initiation at the right moment in all the ways of life and thought and feeling which bind together the tribe. They are the only systems of education I have ever heard of which seem to be beyond improvement.

But when we turn to civilisation it is difficult not to feel contempt for every system, however full of sympathy one may be with the teachers. 'The true teacher must, like the poet, be born, not made,' writes lately an English school-manager, who is a magistrate as well as an academic. But all that our huge and rigid systems of education, which never seem to have any relation to the central facts of life, can do for the born teacher is to crush and extinguish him. No wonder every system is a failure, while at the same time, as an American educational authority grimly remarks: 'Educational reformers have to be a hopeful lot.'

Personally I have never attached much value to any education I was subjected to, but only to the education I voluntarily sought. I sometimes question whether there is any place for education in civilisation. Of course it is essential that systematic knowledge and training should be available; that is another matter. But in view of the general discontent there is at least some ground for concluding that civilisation is incompatible with educational systems.

Under savagery, it is true, such systems are excellent and effective. But with the coming of civilisation the social aim automatically changes. New possibilities of breeding come into view. The prospect opens for bringing into the world only those beings who do not need to be put through the educational mills which worked so well under savagery and are now so widely condemned. Civilisation is essentially a tradition and to be fittingly born into civilization is to absorb that tradition without compulsion.

We still, however, have many savages amongst us.

XXXI

THE YOUNG GENERATION IN AMERICA

A HIGHLY gifted young friend who has lately returned home to America after six years study in European centres, writes from New York: 'I wish there were young people here as enthusiastic and as earnest as some you and I know. I have not met one yet! The best of them are full, not of enthusiasm but of disgust at the charlatanism here, and almost seem to hope for the complete control of government by honest under-world gangsters who don't hide what they are. Merely to start a conversation about the possible improvement of social conditions is to be interrupted by a wisecrack. Anything big is ridiculed by our intelligentsia. In fact the delightful American sense of humour lies in flattening down important things, just as French humour lies in magnifying trivial things.'

I hasten to remark that I do not accept this statement as a complete account of American conditions. Indeed my friend herself is a brilliant example to the contrary. But I have much evidence that it represents the mood of many of the finest young Americans of today. Almost at the same time I receive a letter from another brilliant young American, now completing his training at a European centre whence he will shortly return to the United States.

'Today I am mad with the world,' he writes, 'and impatient with friends. I find so few with the will to live the life within their reach and drink the deep joys the world can offer. It seems a poor race. As my own love of life expands I learn gradually how much one has to feel the deep joys alone. The Lindbergh-baby history has become the symbol of so many things in America; it reads like a colossal uncouth epic of my country. It is all clumsy mass-movement, mass-instinct, and mass-self-destruction.' I may add that my friend was born and raised in the section of New York that Al Capone comes from, and went to school with boys who have become gangsters since.

The attitude of timidity towards life noted by both my friends, the fear of moving except in a crowd, the doubt and scepticism which offend them both, have more justification than they are willing to admit. They are young, of the post-war generation, and were still children during that period of catastrophe. They rebel in part against the old generation which fought the war and is still unfortunately ruling the world, and in part against the spirit of impotent cynicism which that generation has inevitably bequeathed to so many of its offspring in Europe and America.

But if the rebellion against the dominant authority of the war-generation may seem harsh, it is also a promise for the coming time. My friends may criticise post-war America, just as their European contemporaries criticise post-war Europe, but they are themselves the makers of the United States of the future. They represent the young vigorous creative element everywhere to be found in America though the reins are not yet in their hands. If they are tempted to criticise their own country ferociously it is an America which is passing that they have in mind.

The world is for ever new, and America is new with it. True it is that the United States were in the earliest phase spiritually founded, more truly than by anyone else, by a stout-hearted Puritanic Robinson Crusoe, determined to make his own large island self-supporting and separate from all the world, which might go hang for all he cared. He was mightily successful.

But now the world, and America with it, has changed. It has shrunk alarmingly. You can get half way across it in a few hours, when formerly it took two or three months; you can hear, and now even see, what is going on almost anywhere. But in this new America, unfortunately, the old Robinson Crusoe mentality still survives, and is even still in a position to act with crushing force.

That is the situation which young America is perhaps grasping. In so small a world, it is impossible any longer for any country to keep outside and view the rest of the world with supreme indifference. America is beginning to see — and indeed beginning very acutely to feel — that it is itself a part of the world, and when the world suffers will have to suffer with it. Young America finds that it has to take its fair share in ruling the world, not entirely for the world's sake but even more for its own sake.

That seems the direction in which the younger generation is moving. I have only to add that I belong to the old generation which always puts all the obstacles it can in the way of movement.

XXXII

SCIENCE AND ART

A SCHOLARLY correspondent, otherwise unknown to me, writes from Ann Arbor to find fault with my conception of science in relation to art.

'I am reading your *Dance of Life*,' he tells me, 'and would like, if you would permit, to correct some opinions which I think are erroneous. You say that science is an art and the true man of science an artist. This generalisation is too broad to have any validity. Art, to be sure, is like science, creative or imaginative. But the analogy goes no further. Science is practical and art has not the least semblance of practicality. Science responds to such desires as can be satisfied in the external world; Art (*via* poetry, painting, sculpture, etc.), satisfies a residue of frustrated desires which can only be satisfied in an ideal and make-believe world. Art is diametrically opposed to science, and no generalisation can bring them under one heading.'

This is a clear statement of a position which has been widely held, but to me seems to be based on misapprehensions and now out of date. I would even say that my correspondent's definitions of the respective scope of science and art might be reversed and still remain plausible, or rather, I would say, more nearly correct.

All art is of the nature of doing; that is to say that there is no art that is not practical. My correspondent is still under the influence of the old notion that art meant what were called the 'Fine Arts,' which were supposed to be confined to the making of things beautiful to the senses but quite useless. There is no ground for any such distinction. We may have good art or bad art, but all our doing is of the nature of art, and there is no clear line of distinction between art that is useless and art that is useful. It is the same with science. All science is a doing, manual or mental, and even though the greatest men of science have often been indifferent to any uses of their science (just as the conventional artist is supposed to be to his art), unsuspected uses are constantly being found.

'Man is a two-legged reptile,' said Byron, 'crafty and venemous.' That is an unpleasant way of saying that he is a natural artist. Nature indeed is everywhere an unconscious artist, and all animals are in their different ways artists. They are also constantly carrying on science in the practice of their arts. In the choice of the right foods, in the methods of obtaining them, in the construction of their habitations, in the rearing of offspring, and in many more complicated ways that are beyond human comprehension, animals possess what we should call science. Even the dog who swallows meat offhand while he carefully chews a piece of bread has somehow acquired a scientific knowledge which we need a physiological laboratory to make clear.

I do not regard this as a mere idle dispute about words. It seems to me urgent that the superstition still cherished by my correspondent should be dissipated as soon as possible. It is well illustrated by the antagonism still foolishly felt by many people where machinery is concerned.

My correspondent at Ann Arbor would no doubt say that machines belong to the sphere of science and have nothing to do with art. He would be quite wrong. As Jaques

Lafitte, the French engineer and architect, clearly shows in his just published book of 'Reflections on the Science of Machines' (not yet translated into English), machines develop from tools which are undoubtedly works of art, and machinery is becoming ever more closely identified with the supreme art of architecture.

The reason why it is important to unify our notions of what we commonly call 'science' and 'art,' is in order to purify both. We have too long suffered from the narrow conception of an art that may possibly be beautiful but is quite useless, and a science that may be useful but is certainly ugly. Good science is both beautiful and useful, and so also is good art. To be completely so it must be almost instinctive; then we are no longer anxiously concerned with 'works' of art or of science.

'In the end,' Professor Herbert Read, one of our chief authorities on æsthetics, has lately said, 'art should so dominate our lives that we might say: There are no longer works of art, but art only. For art is then the way of life.'

XXXIII

THE APPROACH TO MARRIAGE

A CORRESPONDENT in Minneapolis writes to ask my advice. He has been an inhabitant of the earth, as he puts it, for more than a score of years, and is, he adds, of Caucasian race, and still a celibate. But there has been 'a presidential term of courtship with a member of the opposite sex of the same natal and racial origin,' and he professes 'somewhat serious contemplation of connubial arrangements.' After some further preliminaries he reaches the object of his letter.

'In order to be prepared to intelligently enter into a matrimonial venture, I would value highly your counsel in a pre-marital analytical study and advice as to what course to pursue in order to become thoroughly familiar with biological etc. differences.'

I suppose I must tell him that in the course of that sexual enlightenment which he says he is already pursuing among the shelves of the Central Library there are many excellent books he may possibly find helpful. So far as concerns the non-sexual differences, psychic and physical, I might even venture a modest reference to my own book *Man and Woman*; while for the rest I would certainly commend to him the lately published book by Dr. Exner, *The Sexual Side of Marriage*.

Yet there will be many things left over which I shall not say to him, things which perhaps it may be rather unkind and unwise to say to the celibate bridegroom of twenty-three. I have long been concerned with what my correspondent calls 'sex enlightenments,' and I have nothing to unsay with regard to their high desirability in progressive stages from the earliest years.

Yet I am always, in my own mind, exceedingly well aware that, necessary as are those preliminary 'enlightenments,' they can never take the place of actual experience. Marriage in this respect at all events resembles swimming, in that it is not easy to learn it on a table. It is only by plunging into the waters of marriage or of the sea that one can learn to swim in either element. I am sometimes astonished to find how wonderfully well some people, who seemed to me quite unlikely to be able to achieve it, succeed in swimming in marriage. Men who, by their experience, or the lack of it, and their whole outlook, appeared impossible, somehow succeed triumphantly, and in the end leave widows who worship their memory. Similarly with some women.

But it is by no means always so. It is not indeed always so even with those who approach marriage with what seems the very best preparation.

'We are absolutely incompatible,' writes a friend, a woman physician who entered marriage with what seemed the best possible equipment of knowledge and experience, and is now moreover the devoted mother of fine children. 'I see a great deal in him to love and like, but on the other hand I hate him for not seeming to find anything to like in me.' I hasten to add that my friend, though at times desiring to do so, has not really any serious intention to unmarry.

That brings us to what must ever be the core of the matter. Marriage always is, and even under happy circumstances still remains, what Keyserling calls a *tension*. He calls it indeed a 'tragic tension,' but for that there is no occasion. The tension is not to separate the pair; but to hold them together; it can indeed be a tonic and strengthening bond; it may well be the necessary condition for the finest joys of marriage. Under all its forms, life, to be worth anything, is a discipline. What may be said for marriage is, not that it avoids tension, or escapes being a discipline, but that at the best its rewards are great.

Still I am not sure that it is necessary to say this to my correspondent at the present stage of his connubial arrangements. I will leave him to pursue peacefully the course of the preliminary 'sex enlightenments.'

XXXIV

THE FAMILY PEDIGREE RECORD

A HUNDRED years ago in the wilds of Kentucky an Irishman attached himself to my family in the quality of great grandfather to me. Aside from this temporary interruption, I believe my strain has been strictly American for a couple of centuries and was strictly English before that (on father's side from Geoffrey Clement, one of Charles I's judges, while my mother's family were Lambtons, insignificant people till they became Earls of Durham). But remember I am only telling you what was told me by my parents. I have never felt interested to know whether their volunteered information was sound or not, and I have never inquired into my ancestry on my own account. History teaches that a man can't be too careful about barking up his family tree. He is likely to uncover game up there that is more gamey than he wants.'

When I mention that I received this letter, not today but more than forty years ago, many readers will recognise at once that it was written by Mark Twain. Being interested in the ancestry of notable men, I had asked him to tell me of his, and this was the main portion of his reply, now, I think, for the first time printed.

I am reminded of it today when Dr. Blacker, the able and energetic secretary of the London Eugenics Society, brings for any criticisms I may have to offer the Family Pedigree schedule now being prepared for general use by his Society. It has long been borne in mind that Sir Francis Galton, whom we may regard as the founder of eugenic study, held that every educated person should study his own family pedigree.

The new schedule, however, is worked out on more modern lines than previous schemes. It is now issued to encourage educated people, for their own interest and still more that of their descendants, to prepare a really accurate record of their pedigree and history, more comprehensive as well as more precise than was done of old in the Family Bible. How necessary this is I am myself keenly aware when I recall the difficulties I have encountered in the study of persons of genius, of whom sometimes scarcely even the name of the mother is recorded, or the place of origin of either parent.

As I study this schedule and its accompanying instructions I realise with amusement how antiquated is now the view expounded to me in the last century by Mark Twain.

In the first place one notes the lofty and supercilious tone. He has 'never felt interested,' and for that lack of interest in his own family he evidently pats himself on the back instead of feeling deeply ashamed.

In the second place one notes the dread of finding something 'gamey' up the ancestral tree. One smiles as one realises how different is our attitude in these matters. Today we take almost as much pride in debunking, not only other people but ourselves, as our ancestors seem to have taken in fitting on home-made angels' wings.

How shocked Mark Twain would have been if he could see the Eugenics Society's matter-of-fact instructions that in these records due note is to be taken of addiction to drugs, venereal disease, and conviction for crime. In Victorian days it would have been futile even for a Galton to stress that point.

For my own part I may acknowledge that the remote ancestor I know most about, and feel most interested in — though Mark Twain might have thought him too 'gamey' — was a certain seventeenth century lawyer who spent some time in prison and probably deserved it. My regret is that he never had the opportunity of filling in and handing down to me one of these records.

XXXV

THE RIDDLE OF THE UNIVERSE

A<small>ND</small> by the way: do you think that Man's faculties will ever become sharp enough for him to discover the riddle of the Universe? If you will answer briefly, it will make me very happy.' So ends a letter from a rather young correspondent whose other queries are less formidable.

As I need scarcely say, I do not know, and cannot guess, what Man's faculties will be capable of in the future. But the question suggests trails of thought to one who has at various times thought about the 'Universe.'

In the first place, there are two really quite distinct ways in which we may approach the 'riddle of the Universe,' one scientific, the other religious. It is the latter which has had most personal interest for me, but it seems to be the other, the scientific approach, which has most widespread interest today. As a recent English newspaper discussion has shown, it is astonishing how large a number of educated people take a keen interest in the structure of our Universe. The wide circulation of Sir James Jeans's book on our 'Mysterious Universe' bears witness to the same interest.

For my own part, I have usually been accustomed to resign myself to an attitude towards our Universe corresponding to what I suppose to be that of a philosophic cheese-mite towards 'Our Cheese.' The exact shape and size of our Cheese — I mean our Universe — and whether or not there is anything outside it, have seemed to me questions of a very speculative kind.

But of late, I admit, such questions have assumed a new actuality. The influence of Einstein, putting forth a conception of the Universe which has actually been at some points verifiable, has encouraged others. Various persons, profound and abstruse in astronomy and mathematics — Eddington, Whitehead, Jeans and the rest — have dared to come forward to present their opinions concerning the construction of the Universe. Unfortunately, however, they do not agree among themselves, or always with themselves. So that Einstein, who at one time looked upon the Universe as finite but expanding, is now inclined to withdraw from that position.

What is 'space' and what is 'time'? Is the Universe finite or infinite? Or, as Bertrand Russell once stated, is there no 'Universe' at all? Is space curved? Or is it, as Kant long ago said, just a 'form of the human mind'? Or 'a dream really based on observed reality'? Or 'a metaphysical problem lying beyond the scope of scientific inquiry'? Such are the questions about which those whom we regard as the chief authorities differ widely; while outside the circle of disputing authorities are those inquisitive and intelligent persons who want to know what the authorities mean. How can we picture curved space? Or, an infinite Universe? And if finite and expanding, what is it expanding into?

That is where matters now stand as regards the scientific riddle of the Universe. They still seem to afford some justification for my cheese-mite attitude. But I gladly admit that the fact that the most competent scientific men are now able to put forth such possibilities, and the rest of the world to consider them seriously, indicates a new phase. We are bound to agree with a recent statement by Lord Rayleigh that the science of one generation, however abstruse it may seem, becomes the mere 'common-sense' of the next.

The religious riddle of the Universe stands on a totally different foundation. It belongs not to the sphere of science, though the scientific man is entitled to a voice in it, but to that of emotion. I will not dwell on it here because I have lately done so in the Introduction to a reprint of a book which profoundly influenced me in youth, James Hinton's *Life in Nature*. It influenced me, not by giving me a creed, or making me the disciple of a doctrine, but by furnishing a clue. It enabled me to realise for myself that it is possible to feel that the Universe is not an alien and hostile monster with which one must be ever at war, but the home in which one may be at rest at the centre, whatever troubles one may meet at the surface. The home-feeling of the Universe: that for me is religion.

Others may reach that end by other paths; I have no general prescriptions to offer. But there are some of us whose peace of spirit in the actual world, as well as our practical activity, depends on the possession of a home-feeling in the Universe.

XXXVI

THE SECRET OF SUCCESS

I'LL deeply appreciate if you'll answer this question for me: What do you attribute your success in life to? Please answer the question as I'd like to publish your reply. I thank you in advance and wish you a bright healthy future.'

It is now some little while since I received this demand from an evidently youthful correspondent in New York. But I have from time to time thought about it since.

The reason is that the question presented rather a new problem to me. I was not aware that I had ever consciously aimed at 'success,' nor even considered in what sense, if any, I had achieved it. Further, supposing that on consideration I could reach a precise and definite answer to these questions, would my answer be of the slightest use to anyone else? For it was evident that this was the point my correspondent had in mind.

Speaking only for myself — though I am thereby doubtless speaking for many others — I can only say that what at the outset I sought from the world was not any abstract final 'success' but simply the work that suited me to do. For anyone who is by temperament rather indolent, the main thing is to find something in which he is passionately interested, something which will bring all his special aptitudes into action. That is sometimes difficult; it may take years to find. Diderot, the great French encyclopedist, was a man of the sort I have in mind. As a youth all he could say in

reply to the question what he wished to be was: 'Nothing.'
Yet a little later he was full of devouring energy, and the
lines of thought and action he helped to open out are those
we follow today. He achieved what in the highest sense was
'success,' yet there is not the slightest reason to suppose that
he ever made it, in any personal sense, his aim. As we look
back to his career we do not find him claiming the finest
things he achieved, he was always ready to work for other
people, he spent himself recklessly for any impersonal
cause on which his heart was set. He achieved an immortal
place, if not with complete indifference to personal ends,
still with a main eye on aims beyond himself.

Yet that is not the typical attitude towards life; it is not
even the attitude set forth for imitation in a once famous
book which I read as a boy and with a complete lack of
sympathetic interest, Samuel Smiles's *Self-Help*. For most
young people it may well be that 'success' is the right aim
in life. That is to say to choose some sort of a position which
will be rather difficult to reach, but will enable you to marry
and provide comfortably for your wife and children, to
figure respectably in the public eye, and confer on you the
power of exercising a certain amount of influence on public
life. That is what 'success' usually means, and there is no
reason to regard it as an unworthy aim.

The main difficulty seems to be that this aim is so often
conceived without any just idea of the seeker's real nature,
without any realisation of his aptitudes or his will-power.
So that the youth starts out with the intention of reaching
some high position in business or the State, and in the end
meekly contents himself with a routine of drudgery. 'Success' was for him — it is for so many — merely a dream, a

will o' the wisp, without any relationship to his constitutional possibilities.

It is not indeed so for all. Sir William Gull, a poor boy born in a small cottage such as the ordinary English peasant occupies (I once visited it), made up his mind to become Physician to the King. And the King's Physician in due course he became. I knew a young man who made up his mind to reach a still higher position; circumstances were altogether against him; it seemed an absurd ambition; yet some forty years later he reached it. In such cases we doubtless witness not merely a considerable degree of mental ability but still more of concentrated and self-possessed will-power, impervious to external hindrances, and able to work underground with a constant eye on a secret goal.

For my own part I am more interested in another kind of success, however less worldly and less brilliant. Position is not the only aim in life though it may be the most usual aim. Just the same modicum of ability and just the same patient will-power may be expended on some impersonal object, in the achievement of some difficult work or the solution of some puzzling problem, even when either the work or the problem have by others been passed by, even perhaps as too humble. The success which may crown such an effort, though less dazzling than the other, sometimes transcends all imagined expectation and proves more permanent. Such was Diderot's.

I have always been interested in the adventure of Saul the son of Kish, who went forth to seek his father's asses and found a kingdom.

XXXVII

TOLSTOY

I AM asked to state whether Tolstoy's art and ethics still have as much influence on me as my correspondent seems to believe they once had, and to furnish my opinion as to the extent of the influence of Tolstoy on the younger generation of today. This statement, I am told, together with the opinions of a number of other people throughout the world, is to be forwarded for preservation to the Tolstoy Museum in Moscow.

It hardly seems to me that any opinions of mine regarding Tolstoy are worth embalming for the benefit of posterity. I imagine that posterity will be quite able to form its own opinion, and will view with amusement the opinions of the unenlightened people who went before. Still, if not for posterity's sake at all events for my own, I find a certain interest in trying to discover what my attitude today is towards Tolstoy. I am the more tempted to do so since in the course of my life I have more than once set down my opinion on the matter, and even my earliest book contained a long essay on Tolstoy.

Certainly at that time I took Tolstoy very seriously, not only as a novelist but as a teacher, or at all events as a searcher for truth in the path of life. I had read his *Confessions* and other personal books as carefully as I had read his novels and stories. What deeply interested me, even more than the great artist, was what seemed to me the great man — 'a blind but unconquered Samson' as I described him — struggling in the dark for a gospel he could not grasp. This double aspect made him for me by far the greatest and most interesting figure of his age.

I am not one of those who go out of their way to meet great writers. When the question of meeting one such arose — I no longer recall who it was — I remember the shocked realisation of my friend Arthur Symons at my indifference: 'You would not cross the road to see him!' But Tolstoy I was anxious to meet.

When the time came for a journey to Russia I secured an introduction and much looked forward to the experience. But scarcely more than an hour before the night train was due to leave Moscow, on the date appointed for my visit to Yasnaya Polyana, came to me a letter from Tolstoy: his daughter had suddenly been stricken down by typhoid fever and visitors could not be admitted to the house. Therewith my one chance of meeting Tolstoy was lost.

That was long ago. So much new light has been thrown on Tolstoy since then, alike by the publication of his own and his wife's diaries, and the impressions and conversations of those who knew him, that I have been enabled to revise considerably my original conception of the man.

Tolstoy is today for me, above all, a great artist, as great an artist as the history of the novel has ever shown. Nowhere in fiction can we see life in its essential facts revealed more comprehensively, with a more penetrating insight to the core of things, or with a finer balance and sanity.

Yet, as I see him now, the man who thus transmuted his penetrating observation and turbulent experience of life into those superb forms of art was never himself an artist in life. He struggled, no doubt, but from first to last he fell

into all sorts of mistakes that sometimes were almost child-
ish. From first to last he showed no such judgment in the
real world as in the world of fiction. He never, to the end,
brought love and harmony into even his own household.
He never even to the end brought harmony into his own
soul. In his work we are amazed at the intellectual force
he displayed; in real life his intellectual judgments were
prejudiced, unbalanced, and narrow.

It is reported that Tolstoy did not much care either for
Shakespeare or for Goethe, and it is a significant fact. He
was a very great artist. But he was not among the whole
men. He was not even, where he so much desired to be,
among the holy men.

XXXVIII

MY GARDEN

I WONDER what chance I have of seeing you and your lovely garden,' writes a dear friend, 'or of you coming to see mine. Which reminds me that I have this year spent more trouble over it than ever before, and yet I ask myself: To what purpose since no one is likely to come this summer and see it? for in the present world-depression friends write to say they cannot afford to stir this year. Then I grow sad, for my enjoyment in my garden is largely the enjoyment of sharing it with others. Still I pluck up courage and go ahead with my garden, not only useful vegetables but flowers, though heaps of urgent work await me indoors. Why, when the world is so depressed and ugly? Why, above all, flowers?'

I am not sure that my own garden can be called lovely, and I certainly claim fewer successes than my friend. Things are always going wrong in my garden. It is beset by enemies from above and beneath and all round. In this uncertain English climate either a sudden cold snap in spring destroys all the fruit blossoms, or a sunless summer prevents all but the hardiest fruits from ripening, or a violent storm lays low the most delicate delphiniums, or an early frost turns brown the dahlias just when they were opening, or an unaccustomed drought wilts everything, while I struggle around with a watering-can until the water-supply is exhausted or I am.

But that is not all or even the worst. There are always

the birds. The blackbirds come early and, gazing at me in a cheerful and friendly manner, eat every cherry just before it is ready to gather, so that I have not yet tasted one. Other birds open the pods and eat raw the peas that I should enjoy cooked. Wasps in some seasons bury themselves in the ripening gooseberries or devour the raspberries. I have endeavoured with considerable trouble and expense to cultivate strawberries in a wire cage, since I respect the saying of the ancient wise man who told us that: 'Doubtless God could have made a better berry but doubtless God never did.' The plants are in excellent condition, but (in the enforced absence of birds) insects, slugs, and field-mice have attacked every berry at an early stage and not left one whole. So that here I have not even the consolation of a friend who once worked out complacently the extravagant price which, when all expenses were reckoned up, each of his cabbages represented.

It is true I am not single-handed in the struggle. I am aided from time to time by an ex-service man, disabled by the war, who has taken to gardening, for which he had no training and possesses no natural instinct. He is willing and hard-working; I do not want to discourage him; but I often think that he acquired on the battlefields of France a skill in destruction for which now his only field is my garden.

Yet, notwithstanding all these troubles, I find much joy in my garden. During recent weeks of rare summer weather I have been living in it; I am there at this moment. We have our meals in it; we take sunbaths there. I am pleased to know that my tulips are finer than any to be seen hereabout, and if I attempt to establish an avenue of hollyhocks I am amused to be told by a German friend that Goethe enjoyed a similar pleasure. Every day there is some new spectacle of pleasure or some new difficulty to meet.

When the season grows inclement and I live indoors instead of reclining on the couch of my revolving sun-hut, I still find pleasure in remembering my garden. So it is that I can, for instance, recall visions of my far-away friend, the American dancer who declared that she knew no such dancing-floor as my lawn, and I still seem to see her as the dusk fell and darkness came on, while to the strains of record after record the lithe and lovely figure shone through the gloom until the last floating garment seemed to melt away.

After all a garden is a symbol and a miniature of the world. My friend's problem is easy to solve. In a garden, as in the world, we live to struggle with pains and troubles and out of their midst to snatch our joys.

I should have no difficulty in believing that my first parents were brought up naked in a garden; and that dreams of Paradisaic origin still float in the brains of their descendants.

XXXIX

WE ARE ALL COMMUNISTS NOW!

By the way, why have so many fine people a bee in their bonnet about Russia? Or is it because my pacifist heart revolts at the means employed that I see nothing to thrill me in the Russian enterprise? A vast and bold effort, of course, but is it Communism? And is it easy to see Communism as a possibility in our days, even in Russia where the conditions seem so primitive and favourable? We seem to find there an impetus to internal industrialisation, with crêches and nurseries for the children of women workers. But there are numberless good crêches and nurseries for such mothers in England, yet we do not here regard the ideal society as that wherein every woman is on the level of a factory hand.'

This passage from a letter, just received from a friend, has sent me back to a book of my own published exactly forty years ago and long out of print: *The Nationalisation of Health*. When I turn it up now, it is interesting to observe how largely it is out of date and yet how instructive it remains. It was mainly based on my own early experiences in hospitals and medical practice; it also contained a chapter, gleaned from the most authoritative sources, about contemporary Russian health conditions.

At that time, like many others, I strongly felt that there could be no great civilisation, and never had been, unless where the primary conditions of health are recognised as of the first importance for the community. That they were not so recognised I regarded as 'the chief element of rotten-ness in our civilisation,' and I brought forward a few facts from what I regarded as 'the terrible history of modern England.'

It was to illustrate the argument that I turned to the state of Russia. I described how Russia had the highest birth-rate and the highest infantile death-rate in Europe, so that in some regions nearly seventy children in every hundred died before reaching the age of five; while in country dis-tricts there was less than one doctor to every twelve thousand inhabitants. Even at that, the doctor was often spurned in favour of the witch-doctor who sometimes would not hesi-tate to supply poison for a neighbour's gruel if required.

Typhoid, the epidemic of impure water, raged always and everywhere; typhus, the fever of filth and overcrowding and starvation, found a quarter of a million victims every year. In the factories men and women worked for twelve to fourteen hours a day, and yet could not earn enough to eat; they were often homeless, and sometimes housed, both sexes together at some places, on bare shelves, one above another. All this in spite of careful statistical presentation of the facts and the spasmodic efforts of despotic rulers to improve them.

I brought forward the example of Russia to furnish a con-centrated example of a *laissez faire* method of social life which had once prevailed to some extent in Europe gen-erally, and of which we had not yet, even in England, ex-tinguished the traces, while, half a century earlier, the poverty and filth and pestilential atmosphere of the in-dustrial conditions in Manchester almost recalled Russia.

Today I am even a little amused when I contemplate the

indignation and zeal with which I then championed the cause of national and (as I was careful to make clear) international health. For today not only is the battle won but the argument has become commonplace. Hygiene, the prevention of disease and the preservation of health, has entered into our social system; it is accepted as a matter of course, though we may be far from having carried it to perfection.

It is in historical perspective that we fall short. Or else we should have found it quite right and inevitable that many a Russian Soviet worker may feel in Paradise under conditions so primitive still that the Western European worker has often retired from them as intolerable and found himself nearer Paradise at home.

'We are all socialists now!' a prominent English statesman declared some thirty years ago. The statement was not strictly and technically correct. But in a somewhat similar spirit it is possible for us today to exclaim: 'We are all communists now!'

XL

WHERE ARE THE PROLETARIAT?

A ND this glorification of the proletariat, is it really accomplishing what is claimed for it? I doubt it, more and more. I doubt it, not only as regards the present, but even the future. In what direction are the Russians, and indeed all of us, really moving?' I am quoting the continuation of the letter I have already discussed, and I left this question over because it was too weighty to bring in at the tail.

We hear much today from publicists and propagandists of the 'proletariat.' Most of those, however, who use that formidable word do so in such vague and lofty terms that it is impossible to understand what they mean by it. One has to invent a meaning for oneself. It is true that in the circumstances of the world at the moment we have a class who may so be termed since they are unable to produce anything but offspring, the last thing they ought under those circumstances to produce: the Unemployed. But this is really only a pseudo-proletariat, an accidental result of present world-conditions, not a substantial constituent of any healthy modern society. When in due course they cease to be unemployed, they will feel it an outrage to be termed 'proletarians.'

That leads to a fact which, it seems to me, needs constantly to be rubbed in, for so many intelligent people (I mean people who ought to be intelligent) seem unaware of it. When I was young and still inspired by faith in the possibility of a speedy reformation of the world, I used to be surprised, almost shocked, when talking to the workers of Lancashire to find how stolidly conservative they were, how firmly and quietly opposed to all Radical or Socialist ideas. One need not indeed go further than one's charwoman, even today, to hear scathing denunciations of the idleness and dishonesty of the 'lower classes.'

Every working man's home in England has a best parlour, little used, but set up as a bad imitation of the middle class home which is its possessor's ideal. In his mind there is a similar best parlour into which at his most aspiring moments he retreats. The glorification of the proletariat interests him not at all. If at last he has moved a few inches nearer to the middle-class he will die happy.

Today (more strictly at the end of 1931) the small investors of Great Britain, that is to say the lower and working class, had invested nearly three thousand million pounds, or over two hundred pounds per family. It is easy to see, for those who may know nothing about his ideals, that even on the strictly realistic side the English worker is not tempted to become a Bolshevist. The British 'proletariat' is the stronghold of Capitalism.

It is probable one may speak similarly of America. I am reading Mr. V. F. Calverton's *Liberation of American Literature*, a challenging and stimulating book which ought to find many readers (though I hope they will not agree with all of it), and is no doubt its author's most brilliant achievement so far. Mr. Calverton is one of those who magnify the proletariat and present the doctrine of what has been termed 'materialistic mysticism.' He views it, from a distance certainly, bathed in future glory.

It is all the more significant that he finds no true pro-

letarianism in America, just as I find none in England.
'Our proletariat,' he says, 'is bourgeois-minded. There has
been no proletarian ideology developed here.' He puts this
down to special American frontier conditions, and regards
the 'possibility of possession' as an exclusively bourgeois
ideal, not realising that he has come up to a far more universal fact, even though he recognises the further significant
fact that in the nineteenth century the aristocratic upper
class also tended to approximate to the middle class. Both
upper and lower classes, that is to say, gravitate towards
the central middle class.

Even when we turn towards Soviet Russia it appears that
the same fact may now be illustrated. The 'proletarian
ideology' has not developed even there. An acute Italian
publicist, Carlo Scarfoglio, has just pointed out, after ex-
ploring Soviet conditions on the spot, that what we now
witness is the creation of a bourgeoisie, such as revolutions
have ever tended to produce. The revolutionary breaking
of fetters liberates intelligence; the more intelligent become
the more skilled and the more progressive; the less intelligent sink into a lower and more manual class of workers.
Russian communism is 'congealing into social classes.' In
some Soviet factories now the monthly scale of wages is 200
roubles for the clerk, 180 for the skilled worker, and 120 for
the unskilled. At the same time the workers are investing
their savings in the State Savings Bank and (if they are
not defrauded) will in time become, as elsewhere, a Capital-
ist class.

The new bourgeoisie, which in all countries we are approaching, differs from that inaugurated by the French
Revolution in at least one important respect: it tends to be

all-embracing. Under modern conditions the upper class is no longer a rich and dominating class, and the lowest class is disappearing altogether, for with the evolution of machinery there is no place for the unskilled and resourceless proletarian. There is thus an increased tendency to the formation of a central class and the achievement of a new social solidarity. If we have missed material communism we are at all events acquiring a sense of spiritual communism.

Croce, who is still one of our most luminous and wide-visioned thinkers (however rejected in his own land), believes that to the middle class belongs a unique and peculiar function. It is the class that is drawn from all classes, and so rises above class. In addition to its recognised economic character it 'specially represents spiritual values, reconciling, harmonising, and renewing the economic classes.'

It is probable that we may find the most convincing evidence for that argument in the contemplation of genius. Genius in every field is emphatically a middle-class phenomenon. In the field we are here specially considering, the middle class alone (always of course with individual exceptions) has possessed the intellectual force and the generosity of spirit to see beyond class. It is from the middle class that the brilliant champions of aristocracy have arisen, and today it is to the middle class that the champions of the proletariat, the men of the type of Marx and Lenin, belong. No proletarian, who was not a mere follower, has ever glorified the proletariat.

It was an ancient and excellent piece of advice to clear our minds of cant. Unfortunately we can never do it once and for all, since cant is always assuming new shapes. Once religious cant was the enemy; then it was political cant. Today it is economic cant.

XLI

THE SAVAGES OF EUROPE

I HAVE really a fantastic admiration for the English — not so much the average Englishman as the particular individuals you so often produce in England. I like English forms and traditions though I admit they can be empty shells. I think Englishmen are the nearest approach in our time to the Greek ideal of a gentleman. You English are something to look up to and admire. I am glad of it. If I could not find something better than myself I would go and look for it.'

I am quoting from a letter of a one hundred per cent American, though at present he is not living either in America or in England. It will be said to reveal what the fashionable psychoanalytic slang of the day calls the inferiority complex, which Americans often like to claim, if not for their individual selves at all events for fellow-countrymen.

I do not bring forward my friend's letter in order to express an opinion one way or the other. It is true I have often been a severe critic of the Anglo-Saxon at many points, but when it comes to final estimates I have nothing to say. One cannot get outside one's own skin or sever oneself from one's own blood, and to presume to express an opinion about one's own national goodness or badness seems — if I may be allowed to put it too mildly — ridiculous. Yet it remains all the more interesting to study the opinions of outsiders.

In 1804 Julie Talma wrote to Benjamin Constant: 'You

make me shudder, my friend.' She had just heard that Napoleon is in danger of falling into the hands of the English. 'It is certain that the English do not belong to the class of civilised peoples. I do not even think they belong to the human species.'

Writing in the same year, though in Berlin, the Comte de Tilly, whose fascinating *Memoirs* have now at length appeared in English, spoke in exactly the same tone. Indeed his language was so abusive that when, twenty years later, the *Memoirs* were at last published in France, these passages were omitted, since public feeling had changed, and they have never been printed in their original French, though they now appear in English.

Lately I secured a rare little book which is full of interest in the present connection. It is dated 1764 and is entitled *The Savages of Europe*. These, I need scarcely say, are the English, and the book is a translation of a French original which had appeared two years earlier, and is attributed to a writer, now forgotten, called Lesuire. The book would have had more wit and vivacity if it had come from the pen of the author's contemporary, Voltaire, but as Voltaire was an outspoken Anglophile that could not be hoped for.

The frontispiece to the volume represents a wolf flourishing a carving knife in his forepaw in front of a table laden with a huge joint of beef, a plum-pudding, and a big tankard, the Englishman's traditional fare. The story tells how an estimable young Frenchman accompanied by his virtuous future bride, weary of the chatter and scandals of French life, crosses the Channel, eager to enjoy happiness in the land of philosophers. They meet at once a wise and benevolent old Chinaman, Kin Foe, who feels it his mission to reform savages everywhere, and after spending some time among 'my old friends the Caribees' has just arrived to carry on a similar task in England. From the very first all three of these innocents abroad meet with brutality, insult, fraud, and outrage. They are thrust into familiarity with Newgate and Tyburn and the worst scoundrels in London, barely escaping with their lives; indeed the old Chinaman actually succumbs to his injuries, and the lovers set sail back to France 'with firm but unnecessary protestations of never revisiting the abominable asylum of the savages of Europe.'

What I read with sympathy, in this scarcely brilliant little volume, is the translator's 'Advertisement,' as he calls his Preface. He is nameless, but a pencilled note on the flyleaf of my copy gives his name as J. P. Andrews. He had chanced to pick up the book, he tells us, during a tour on the Continent, 'was struck with the humour of it, and took it into his head that, though in the satire the failings of Englishmen are exaggerated beyond all reason, yet it might, on the whole, be of some use to his countrymen to know in what light they are seen by foreigners.'

The translator's judicious moderation is, indeed, delightful. He certainly finds 'a few anachronisms' in the book and points these out. If the author lies at times, he remarks, 'he had a kind of right to make us accountable for abuses so very lately rectified,' and if, as in regard to priesthanging, he is quite wrong as to English practices, he still 'has the letter of the law on his side.' There could not be a more temperate retort to almost unqualified abuse. I hope I may count Mr. J. P. Andrews as a fairly typical Englishman.

It remains true, as my friend remarks in the letter I quoted at the outset, that 'there is no point in wasting time by looking on oneself with satisfaction.' Still there is a certain amount of amusement in contemplating the varying attitudes of other people.

XLII

THE DESIRE FOR POSSESSION

'I HAVE tamed a thrush, a fascinating little creature, friendly, and full of gentle chatter when she comes rather near,' writes a woman friend from whose letters I have before quoted. 'I was almost moved to tears. Yet I see in her so nakedly the primitive natural instincts: jealousy and the desire of possession. My thrush displays a ferocious temper towards any intruding bird which dares to approach her tame ogre (as I imagine she might consider me). There are two little robins also beginning to become friendly, and this increases the difficulty, for these two little devils are jealous of each other, while the thrush is ready to pounce on either if found within her territory. For nearly an hour my robins will patiently watch the same crumb which neither gets, for any near approach leads to a fight, and a wild flight round the garden; or the thrush drives both away and carries off the spoil. Do we see here those passions of jealousy and possession which among mankind today Revolutions, political or moral, are organised to overcome?'

I am interested in my friend's ornithological observations because they chance to come exactly to the point of reflections I have myself been making. In reading Mr. Calverton's *Liberations of American Literature* I found it stated, I confess with some surprise, that the desire for possession is a characteristic of the bourgeois middle class. Yes, I said to myself, without doubt; and, equally without doubt, it is a characteristic of the low-class proletarian, and, again without doubt, of the upper-class aristocrat. Going further abroad, it certainly without doubt marks the whole human species. Now my friend's observations suggest the further reflection that it is a characteristic of animal life generally. It is really possible, I am now inclined to say, to go still further, and invoke the ecologist who will probably admit that it also marks plant life; though here the biological fact has no demonstrable psychic manifestation.

So the conclusion emerges that we are face to face with one of the ultimate facts of life. We may calmly bear that in mind when we hear such political or moral slogans as 'Property is theft!' or 'Jealousy is the very devil!' All life is a craving for possession, and jealousy is merely the crude instinct to guard that craving and to defend possessions. It is a mistake to suppose that any socialist or communist order of society alters that fundamental fact.

Certainly the world has seen many Revolutions, but, as even those who make Revolutions quickly discover, human nature remains the same. The same stolid old human passions still work in exactly the same way. All that has happened has been some readjustment of possessions among individuals or among classes. On that slightly modified foundation things are soon working exactly in the same routine as before. That is why the idealist always looks so sadly on the Revolution he has sacrificed himself to bring about, or at all events would, if he was not himself so often destroyed in its achievement.

Yet the modified foundation may really be an improvement. By curtailing the possessions of the upper social layer, or increasing the possessions of the lower social layer, it may enlarge the sum of happiness in the community. It is important to realise that this foundation can be secured, and is in fact in some countries being secured, by gradual social transformation, without any revolutionary appeal to impossible slogans, and without the misery which the unduly swift attempt to realise those slogans always involves.

As the world is made, any escape from the mania of possession is reserved, not for the proletarian masses, but for the elect few. I have elsewhere argued (harmonising the arguments of two distinguished thinkers, Jules de Gaultier and Bertrand Russell) that there is such an escape. It is possible to replace the joy of possession by the joy of creation, and to sublimate the material desire of grasping things into the æsthetic pleasure of contemplating them. There are always some rare and choice spirits for whom this is a possibility. And their very presence among us has added to the well-being of those who can only in part and occasionally imitate them.

They remain the few. The vast bourgeois middle class of our planetary world will continue to be represented by the thrushes and the robins in my friend's garden.

XLIII

THE EFFICIENCY OF MIXED RACES

You possibly remember the remark of a Californian teamster who was remonstrated with for objurgating his refractory mule with unnecessary severity. "Yes," he said, "but you see what riles me is that the derned fool seems to forget everything but the *hoss* side of his ancestry!" A wholesome belief in the efficiency of mixed races might have saved him from this dangerous conceit. I have possibly escaped it by not clearly knowing in my own mind which was the *hoss* side of mine!'

That is not from a letter of today. Far from it! It was written in 1887 by Bret Harte, then living in London, in response to an inquiry of mine concerning his ancestry. He told me that, to the best of his knowledge, his mother was descended from the early Dutch settlers in America, while his father was distinctly English. Hence the doubt in his mind.

This question of the comparative virtues of races is one of those great disputes which are always rising up afresh and stirring violent passions. It should be a calm scientific problem. But it becomes a battlefield between prejudices, with would-be scientific facts flaunted provocatively on each side.

Who has not heard of the great claims made for the 'Nordic' race, and the opposing claims of the 'Latin' race? Or of the contest between long heads and round heads? Yet these 'races,' supposed to be so distinct and so superior or so inferior, all belong to one little corner of the world called Europe. They are too closely allied and too blended together to be properly distinguished as 'races,' while the criteria of race until recently accepted are now considered fallacious. They are today being superseded by the criteria of blood-types which are now being investigated. Race is being determined by the blood group which can only be decided by experiment. When an impartial Japanese scientist comes along and applies serological tests (as he has lately done) he finds that the peoples of Europe are not really different races at all, they are too closely related, though when we go further afield he admits that Eskimos, Kalmucks and Negroes may fairly be recognised as belonging to distinct races. The combatants on both sides have been, as Saint Paul would have put it, fighting as one that beateth the air.

That does not, of course, prevent variations of character in peoples springing from the same racial foundation. There are, moreover, legitimate differences of opinion between those who hold that it is better to be of unmixed descent and those who are in favour of mixture. I am myself in favour of mixture, though not exclusively, such a mixture as, we see, Bret Harte exemplified, even if we do not accept his implied assumption that one hereditary line must be of superior value to the other. It is, I should say, the union of unlike good elements on both sides that counts in achieving superiority.

Long ago I was able to illustrate this point in the study of British genius. Not only was the large general proportion of eminent persons of mixed ancestry here brought out, but many special points were made clear. Thus, while Scotland has contributed far more than her share to the total genius, the Irish and the Welsh have proved better adapted for crossing with the English than the more closely related Scottish, who in an English mixture have produced comparatively little genius. The English and Irish blend stands indeed at the top of all British blends, being only second to the general British and foreign European mixtures which are over thirty-two per cent of all mixtures, English and French coming first in this group. It is noteworthy that blending is specially favourable to the production of high ability in women, as many as thirty-two per cent of eminent British women being mixed, as against thirteen per cent of eminent British men. I am convinced that the same conclusions could be reached in a still more marked degree by an exploration of American genius.

Let me add that in thus proclaiming the virtues of what Bret Harte called 'the efficiency of mixed races,' I have no personal axe to grind. I am myself intensely English, in the ancient and narrow sense, as far back as I can definitely trace, which is for several centuries, though I am pleased to know that it is, to an unusual extent, English of the sea. My temptation is to view with contempt all those miscellaneous hybrids who presume to call themselves 'English.'

XLIV

SCOTT'S NOVELS

MY past opinion of Scott's novels was that they were interesting in parts but frightfully slow and long-winded, so as not to bear re-reading and leaving no distinctive impression behind. My present opinion is that they were spoilt by two things: first by being largely unrelieved history, and second by the pompous style, full of what is now called jargon, of which the most common form is saying in ten words what could be said in two.'

The centenary of Sir Walter Scott's death has brought his name much to the front. The foregoing passage is from a letter of a young friend whom I had asked for his own reaction to Scott's novels. He is sixteen years of age, and I wished to compare his attitude with my own half a century earlier.

I was eleven or twelve years old, and my mother had brought us to the Isle of Wight to spend the holidays by the sea. Almost on arrival she asked the landlady if she had any books to lend me. That worthy woman — blessings on her spirit! — succeeded in producing the early edition in three volumes of *Woodstock*. I had so far only read Scott's epic poem of *Marmion*, which was in our family library, and the novels were unknown to me.

I was introduced into a new world. Here were times and scenes and figures I vaguely knew about from history appearing before me in vivid life. Here romance and realism and humour were generously blended by a mighty hand in a great stream of narrative which bore me along with perpetual delight. All the elements in literature which appealed to me were here combined, and there were none too subtle or too remote for my youthful spirit to grasp.

On returning home I soon discovered the best cheap edition of Scott's novels, and on many a Saturday that followed during my schoolboy years my weekly pocket money was spent on a Scott novel. As I had to space out these purchases, I would sometimes with undiminished delight re-read one of my favourites. But I secured most of them and read each with immense satisfaction, though there were some in which I specially revelled. *Ivanhoe* and *The Abbot* stand out in memory; Catherine Seyton was my adored heroine, and after her Di Vernon.

That went on for some four years. I well remember the end. I was sixteen; I had just arrived in Australia bringing with me *The Pirate*. But for the first time I found Scott tedious. With an effort I finished the book, but I knew I should never again open a novel of Scott's. I never have.

The time had come for George Eliot's *Middlemarch* and Flaubert's *Madame Bovary* and Stendhal's *Le Rouge et Le Noir*, and an endless series of novels English and French and Russian. I was leaving the world of romantic traditions and facing new problems of life and art of which the genial and robust Scott knew nothing and cared less.

When from this point I looked back I could only view Scott critically. I saw that his historical scholarship was shallow and careless, that he was an adept at pastiche, too swift and too copious not to be slovenly at times, that he was conventional in sentiment and rigid in proprieties, while his literary style was sometimes as bad as possible, though that, indeed, could be said of many a great novelist.

Today I view Scott with more balanced judgement. His faults were many and his inequalities disconcerting; but the same may be said, I find, of the very different virtues and vices of the most modern men, D. H. Lawrence, or whom you will.

Scott's work is the outcome of a rich and generous personality endowed with an eager imaginative receptivity. When he appeared he brought into the world what was, in effect, with all its imperfections, a new vision of the panorama of human life on earth. It has ceased to thrill by its novelty. But when it appeared it appealed mightily to grown men and women, and influenced the course of literature everywhere. Half a century ago it was still a Paradise for the young. And now?

Well, it remains a source of joy if you have the fine thirst to drink there. You may take it or, like my young friend, leave it.

I may here point out that, shortly after this was written, Professor G. M. Trevelyan, who speaks with authority as himself a distinguished historian, made clear that Scott was something more than the introducer of the historical novel. He renewed history itself. He brought into it a vitality it had not possessed before. The difference between Gibbon and Macaulay is a difference largely due to the influence exerted by Scott.

XLV

THE MAKING OF GODS

PARDON me for asking your valuable consideration for the claims of a religious system which may reasonably be described as "Naturalism."' So writes a correspondent in London who encloses an elaborate summary of this new and yet old religion.

'In our too artificial civilisation,' writes my correspondent, 'no due attention has been paid to those ancient Deities who have so profoundly affected many peoples, especially the Greeks and Romans, and enabled them to reach such high stages of culture. We pigeon-hole them as classical figures or dismiss them as heathen idols, still moved by as ignorant a spirit as those early Christians who threw down their altars. But surely the time has come when we may rise to a more intelligent and a more worshipful appreciation of those supreme figures of the ancient Pantheon, Apollo, Venus, Eros, Ceres, and Bacchus. I name those who were concerned with the two supreme human functions of Reproduction and Sustentation.'

It may be added that my correspondent demands that votaries of these deities should first pass through the stage of Initiation, and even then not be necessarily eligible for any position in the hierarchy, which comprises nine stages from Doorkeeper up to Supreme Pontiff. It is also proposed to constitute four Companies to deal respectively with Rites, Discipline, Doctrine, and Propaganda.

The founder of this system is not a novice in the search for the Holy Grail. He has been a lifelong seeker after a home of the spirit. He has passed through the Anglican Church; he has entered the Catholic Church; he has come out of it; and in these spiritual adventures he has suffered great loss.

Now at length, it seems to him, he has found what he sought in a renovation of the ancient classic cult adapted to the needs of the present.

While not antagonistic to Christianity and ready to embrace whatever gracious gifts it has to bestow, he feels that Christianity is not wide enough for all the religious needs of today. The ideals of asceticism have ceased to have spiritual value for most people; the ardours of Puritanism have grown pale. There is a new recognition of the natural world; even the shame-faced horror of the body is out of date, and this new prophet welcomes the aid of the nudists with their claim for air and sunshine, and their refusal to accept the blind worship of clothes.

I am reminded of a remarkable passage in Proust where the invalid hero of his famous book, emerging from seclusion, gazes at the wine-merchant's daughter at the cashier's box and the washerwomen gossiping on the pavement, and is filled with the emotion experienced at the revelation of Goddesses. 'For since Olympus has ceased to exist,' he says, 'its inhabitants live on the earth and when a painter would depict a mythological scene, and for Venus or for Ceres goes to the people exercising the commonest trades, far from committing a sacrilege he is restoring to them the quality and attributes of which they have been deprived.'

Perhaps, after all, the forces of civilisation have been working together to prepare the way for our new prophet. The ideals of the immediate past are fading. Nature and Matter, which were once of the Devil, are now seen as instinct with a mystery which is almost or quite divine. Here science and art speak with one voice.

'The universe is a machine of which the essential function is to make gods.' So Bergson declares in the great work by which he has now at last crowned his life-work in philosophy. Religions will never cease to spring forth, in new life or re-newed life.

Does our prophet of Naturalism possess the magic wand so to strike the human heart that the stream of faith shall gush forth? That I may never live to know.

XLVI

THE GOAL OF SCIENCE

'I confess to a certain amount of fiendish pleasure in occasional "bomb-throwing." I find some very simple statements looked upon as bombs.'

This is not the declaration of a Gorgouloff, but comes from the letter of an excellent American woman who happens to think and act in rather more direct and natural ways than the small rural community in which she lives. Her bombs cannot have a wide repercussion.

On occasion, however, some eminent personage or other seems to find pleasure in throwing across the world a far-resounding bomb. Sir Alfred Ewing, a distinguished engineer, lately took advantage of his election as President for this year of the British Association for the Advancement of Science to throw such a bomb at our vaunted civilisation which he has himself contributed to further. It is not necessary to quote here his widely reported pronouncement. But there may be some interest in considering its significance.

Ever since the old faith in Progress died down, with its short cut to human perfection, Civilisation had been liable to attack. This came mostly from, as it were, the outside. Edward Carpenter, one of the finest and sweetest spirits produced by the once despised Victorian period, wrote on 'Civilisation: Its Cause and Cure,' and lived the simple unconventional creed he taught. He admitted, we see, the possibility of a 'cure.' It seemed to him that civilisation could be in a large measure dispensed with. Ruskin and William Morris cherished rather similar ideals, which still my friend William Lloyd carries out in California.

But today the attack on civilisation comes not merely from those who seek, not always successfully, to live outside it. On the contrary it comes from those who are at its most active centre in mechanical science. That is why it is so serious.

A generation ago physical science spoke with a cocksure voice. A big bomb was thrown among pious Victorians when Tyndall from his Presidential chair at the British Association declared that he discerned in Matter and the philosophy of Materialism a mighty promise for the future. Today science only gropes there in a half-light and discerns at the most but shadows and symbols.

But there is more than that to it. While the vision of science has grown dimmer, the technical mastery of science has grown vastly greater. By virtue of insight and laborious patience, men of science have discovered and so harnessed and tamed natural forces that by scarcely more than pressing a button they can be set in action, beneficent or devastating, by millions of the savages living in civilisation who know nothing of the arduous discipline which those must pass through who bring these mighty forces within human reach.

That is the situation which has brought to Ewing a sense of disillusion and alarm. When he now watches the sweeping pageant of discovery and invention in which, he admits, he once took unbounded delight, a wonder seizes him about its goal. It is a modern affair. A century ago it had no existence. Today it is already scattering all over the earth capacities and powers previously unknown and even un-imagined. What is Man going to do about it?

So far, as we know, Man has for the most part been too eager to enjoy the immediate pleasant results to look at the potential tragedy beyond. It is only today, indeed, that he even realises that this comfortable facility in production is itself a tragedy if he has no notion how to organise it for the benefit of all, and is reduced to the imbecile device of burning his cotton and throwing his coffee in the sea and burying his gold in vaults, when half of the race are tortured by the fear of perishing from lack of such commodities.

Mechanical production with its immense facilities is taking the place of human labour. The workman is becoming comparatively unnecessary; the joy of craftsmanship is going. The world is automatically glutted with commodities, and Man, deprived of the old duty to work, knows nothing but to starve. The only alternative he sees is to destroy. By self-discipline, by world-organisation, he could with his new acquired powers bring the earth back to the gates of Eden. But those same powers, without discipline and organisation, enable him to bring it to the gates of Hell. Man is still completely unprepared and unfit for his new responsibilities.

I do not indeed myself admit here an unqualified pessimism. I recall that it is exactly two hundred years since an obscure Italian whose name still slips from memory, invented the pianoforte, neglected at its origin, and today giving scope to the expressive powers of a Schnabel. The vastly complicated instrument now invented by science may well need a couple of centuries before we know how to play on it harmoniously. But at present the last word rests with Ewing:

'The command of Nature has been put into Man's hands before he knows how to command himself.'

It has taken a long time, but we seem to see at length the real significance of the pregnant question of old: 'What shall it profit a man if he gain the whole world and lose his own soul?'

XLVII

THE NEW ARISTOCRACY

THE voice of the people hardly now seems to be the voice of God, but much more like the braying of a donkey. Not that democracy is thereby invalidated. A country mainly inhabited by donkeys should, and must be, governed by donkeys and for donkeys.'

It is a woman, once an ardent suffragette, who puts forward this justification of democracy. But it represents a growing conviction, not less among leaders of thought than among leaders of action.

Half a century ago the democratic ideal still prevailed amongst the finest spirits. John Stuart Mill, whose mind was so well balanced and his vision so wide, continued to exert influence. Karl Marx aroused enthusiasm by his systematic justification of the masses and his prophecy of their ultimate triumph. William Morris put similar ideals into poetic visions. Walt Whitman came forward, a robust and unconventional figure, shocking many but uncompromising in his glorification of the 'common man.' Edward Carpenter in a similar spirit sang of *Towards Democracy*. The worship of Labour with a capital — preferably in its lowest forms of manual work — became almost an epidemic mania.

We have to go rather low today to find the echoes of those voices. These ideals have been, if not exactly realised, at all events vulgarised into sadly deformed shapes. We witness a new orientation of the human spirit. Not that there is any desire to crush the 'masses' — no doubt the democratic ideal has left its wholesome mark — but no serious thinker now looks there for any sort of human salvation.

The potent influence of Nietzsche seems to have played a subtle part in corroding the old ideal. Not that he advocated any definite alternative. But he was disdainful of accepted notions. He had a way of probing into things, and somehow, after he had probed, the things never looked quite the same as they had looked before. And then his Over-Man, however fantastic a figure, seemed to make ridiculous any attempt to kow-tow to the mass-man.

Today Professor Ortega y Gasset seems a typical representative of the intellectual attitude, as may be seen by his recently translated book, *The Revolt of the Masses*. That 'revolt' is a vertical invasion of barbarians, he argues, not advancing from beyond the frontiers of civilisation, but surging up in our midst.

Ortega, it must be remembered, is not an old-fashioned reactionary, clinging to the past and railing at the aspirations of the workers. He is one of the fathers of the Spanish Revolution, from of old a moderate Republican, who did much to bring about the New Spain, and he supports the present Spanish government, though he may not approve of all its actions. The 'classes' he has in mind are not the old 'upper' and 'lower' classes. He means the people of minus quality (to be found among the rich even if more frequently among the poor) and the people of plus quality.

The low class man is he who makes no demands on himself. The high class man is he who disciplines himself to the service of great ends beyond himself. He possesses the creative mind to raise society above the level of commonplace. The mass-man, on the other hand, proclaims the sacred rights of the commonplace, standardises it, and eliminates the creative minority whose work he yet accepts as a matter of course. Here we have the doctrine of the New Aristocracy.

The interesting part about it is that it is ceasing to be only a doctrine. It is becoming a fact of actual government. Half a century ago Matthew Arnold described Parliaments as the homes of clap-trap. He was not taken seriously, for he was what would now be called a highbrow. But the truth he stated has become too glaringly true to be put aside. Parliaments are being dealt with by men who adopt, however less dramatically, the methods of Cromwell, autocrats if not aristocrats. In Italy there is Mussolini, and in Russia Stalin, who may indeed be, as Trotsky said, 'the most prominent average man in our party,' but is at all events an autocrat, ruling an inverted Tsardom with a rod of iron.

And now, in our English speaking world, the Premier of South Africa, General Hertzog, declares that the future of civilisation must not be delivered up to democracy, since the average level of intelligence is not high enough, and there is no ground to believe that the mere extension of education can raise the intellect of a country or eliminate self-interest.

He might have been a student of Ortega y Gasset! It was the dream of Plato that the philosopher and the leader of men be one and the same. Are we approaching that ideal?

'The characteristic of the hour is that the commonplace mind, knowing itself to be commonplace, has the assurance to proclaim the rights of the commonplace and to impose them wherever it will. As they say in the United States, "to be different is to be indecent." The mass crushes beneath it everything which is excellent, individual, qualified, select. Anybody who is not like everybody and does not think like everybody runs the risk of being eliminated.' So Ortega y Gasset in *The Revolt of the Masses*. It is characteristic of the irresponsible and non-proletarian champion of the proletariat to be able to find nothing but vituperation for the man who so speaks; it is also pathetic.

Hertzog is the responsible representative of the mass-man, the elect of democracy, a man whose high character and ability are generally recognised. What he had to say, therefore (in addressing old Stellenbosch students in Pretoria on the 9th September, 1932) is significant: 'I do not share (he said) the optimism of those who hold that we may trust the welfare of our future and of our civilization unconditionally to twentieth century democracy. No one could close his eyes to the fact that the average intelligence of European people is not high, and that thus far there is no justification for accepting the doctrine that an extension of education among all classes is tantamount to an improvement in the intellect of the community, or contributes materially to the elimination of self-interest in democratic institutions. This self-interest has always caused the decline of democracy and civilization throughout history, and will exercise its fatal influence in this century unless it is combated.'

XLVIII

RE–DISCOVERING THE BIBLE

Will you, by the way, please explain your reference to "Gadarene swine"? I am sorry, but I am not familiar with classical literature.'

So writes the German translator of an essay of mine, stumped by this obscure allusion which to me had seemed transparent.

I hastened to reply that the reference is not classical, but could be fully explained by turning to the Gospel of Saint Mark, chapter V, verses 9 to 13, though the 'Gadarene' of the old English Bible is rendered 'Gerasene' in the more correct Revised Version.

I have often enjoyed bringing forward the swine which were possessed by demons and rushed down a steep place into the sea. I find them symbolic of many human situations. The Bible, so full of these significant symbols, has been familiar to me since childhood, though not as a subject of school instruction. After the age of puberty, indeed, I put it aside, drawn by a thirst for more modern literature. Four years later, enriched by new personal experiences, I spontaneously turned to the Bible again. But this time I came to it with a completely fresh vision. Here was no longer for me a supernatural guide-book, but a literature, or rather two literatures. And I found a wisdom and insight deeper and wider than any dogmas could yield. I found as well, even with surprise, a subtlety of art which now seemed to me the secret of the fascination by which it had held the world so long.

That vision might be personal and not for everyone. But I have always regarded the Bible as — for whatever reasons — so well known that it might safely furnish allusions and cadences and echoes without need of chapter and verse. For the Bible is a book — as we commonly call what is really a great collection of books — with a circulation far beyond any other. Last year, indeed, it beat all records by its issue; to be exact, 10,552,284 volumes of Bibles, Gospels, and Psalters were issued by the British and Foreign Bible Society. In England alone the Bible proved a best-seller for the year to the extent of considerably over a quarter of a million copies, while it circulates in 900 languages throughout the world, except in the Soviet Republics.

Yet in one's own circle, wherever the circle may be, do people today read the Bible? There are many who doubt it. Only yesterday an English Bishop was reported as declaring that 'the Bible is quite certainly not read as much now as it used to be. I am confident that people generally are not reading the Bible as their forefathers did.'

I cannot say that I am surprised, but I have no wish to join the clergy in a Bible-reading propaganda. On the contrary I see that it is the very insistence on the Bible, the mere fact of its reckless propagation, which has proved fatal. Indeed, I expect to hear of more eager readers of the Bible in the Soviet Republics than in any other region of the world.

There are many infuriating aspects to modern education. One such specially arouses my own fury. That is the widespread custom of introducing into the schoolroom, to be thumbed by innocent children, the sublimest works of human imagination. Little is thought of reducing to the level of mere schoolbooks Shakespeare and Marlowe and Milton, to sicken children (and teachers themselves often as innocently ignorant) who as yet can know nothing of the naked ecstasies and anguish which are here expressed and transformed in redeeming shapes of immortal beauty.

The Bible, for those who truly know it, is among such works of divine art, and it is the Bible, above all, which is thrust on to children who would find far more spiritual nourishment, if not in Hans Andersen's fairy tales, at all events in books of natural history such as K. de Schweinitz's *How a Baby is Born.*

Where the superior officials are found who, against the judgement of many of the best teachers, ordain that children should acquire a lifelong disgust for great literature and all that it can yield, I do not know. But until they are mercifully confined in Homes for Mental Defectives the world is not likely to 're-discover the Bible.'

Meanwhile the mind dwells on those Gadarene swine, possessed by devils, educational or other, which ran down a steep place into the sea and were choked.

XLIX

THE PLACE OF THE PARENT

I HAVE a personal problem to solve which is causing me much anxiety and unhappiness. Unfortunately I have no parents to whom I can turn for advice and no other friends whose judgement I feel inclined to trust.'

The writer is a young Englishman in a remote part of the world. He mentions that he is about to marry. What his problem is I have no notion.

Yet this letter suggests several reflections. My correspondent supposes that I receive 'hundreds of letters of this sort.' But why should I, a private person, even though willing to give such helpful advice as is in my power, receive such letters? I ask myself what sort of a civilisation it is in which so haphazard a way of obtaining aid in solving the problems of life is the only one available. It is clearly not in the interest of the community that its members should have their best energies hampered by anxiety and unhappiness in front of what may be the central facts of life; or that they should encounter the risk of doing injury not only to themselves but to their social group through the lack of what seems so obvious a resource. Why are there not organised institutional centres where information and advice may be confidentially obtained on intimate questions which may not be strictly and exclusively within the fields of religion or medicine or law, and yet may be on the frontiers of any or all of these fields?

Perhaps, after all, I am only asking what many are beginning to ask and some attempting to answer. In the old days of Christendom there was always the Church, and the Church was prepared to deal with all human problems. That is no longer possible. On the one hand the circle of human problems has spread too wide, and on the other there is no general acceptance of the Church's authority. Some other tribunal is felt to be necessary.

Certainly the secret difficulties which may thus be experienced at some turning-point in life may be of widely different kinds. There is no handbook that can cover them. Often, indeed they have some connection with the physical or psychic aspects of love, which is still the subject more than any other shrouded in secrecy, though now it is so ostentatiously discussed, even in the newspapers.

The Sexual Institute which Dr. Magnus Hirschfeld founded some years ago in Berlin was, indeed, a fine pioneering attempt to answer a part of this deeply felt need. It was admirably planned to give personal information and advice in various departments all more or less concerned with the psychic or physical sciences associated with the human reproductive life. If, in the working out, this Institute failed to prove satisfactory to all parties, it cannot be said that its conception or the splendid generosity of its founder was at fault. On the contrary we are bound to hope that in due course all great centres in every country will possess such Institutes carried on by expert hands with State or Municipal support.

In the Child Guidance Clinics, the foundation of which we owe to the United States, though they have now spread far beyond, we have another attack on this same problem from a different side. In a sense it is a more fundamental approach. If it is good, even late in life, to receive a helping hand when in intimate difficulties, is it not still better earlier? When parents and guardians bring their difficult children to find the skill and care they do not know how to exercise un- aided, there will be fewer unhappy homes and less risk of adults later experiencing more serious troubles.

We see an attempt to meet the problem, for those who have lived long enough to make mistakes, in the establish- ment of that entirely modern kind of judicial machinery usually called Juvenile and Domestic Relations Courts, known throughout the world since the Denver Court was in 1899 set up by the efforts of Judge Ben Lindsey, to whose inspiration we owe the general recognition of the need for such institutions: a machinery, as described by Lindsey, for a human readjustment to life of those who have erred, in place of the old remedies of retribution and punishment. 'The human artist has succeeded the executioner.'

The majority of criminals and delinquents are between the ages of seventeen and twenty-one. That is to say that they are still at an age when the absence of watchful parents or wise friends can be most severely felt. I do not suppose that my correspondent is likely to become a criminal. But he illustrates a great social need. He emphasises the importance of new social institutions only now beginning to arise among us.

L

IS WAR THE BEST WAY OF KILLING?

You make a statement which really quite startled me when you say that the abolition of capital punishment may still be desirable, but that to regard it as a reform that is urgent would be ludicrous if it were not pathetic.'

My correspondent is an active publicist who for thirty years past has advocated the complete abolition of Capital Punishment. I can quite sympathise with him because (as he reminds me) I have myself been in favour of the abolition of the death penalty for an even longer period.

But, as I would like to make clear to my correspondent and others, this seems to me a matter of a just perspective.

We sometimes hear people who know little of the meaning of words talk about the 'sacredness' of life. But there is nothing 'sacred' about life. Or, if we choose to think that there is, we must also admit that death is equally 'sacred.' For they are certainly both on the same level, both alike rooted deep in Nature. As far back as we can trace our zoological history, the aptitude for life and the aptitude for death have been in our hands. The two aptitudes go together; without life there would be no death, and without death no life. Whether we choose to call them 'sacred' or 'secular,' they are most assuredly natural. Each creature gives life to its own species and maintains it by giving death to other living things, animal or vegetable, usually of another species, though occasionally, like Man, even of his own species. When that process stops, Nature, as we know it, will be no more. Meanwhile there is the power to direct it. And never has any species possessed so much power in both directions as Man today.

That is why this question is a matter of perspective. We inflict death, we inflict life (for it often is in every sense an infliction): at what point should we do so with greatest energy?

Capital punishment was once inflicted in so outrageously unjust and copious a way that reform was here urgent. Three centuries ago even the finest members of the community, if they offended the opinion of the gross majority, were liable to be sent out of life. Even a century ago so trivial were the offences for which the penalty was death that numberless young creatures, who might later have been passably good citizens, were prematurely hanged.

Today, in every country, by miscarriage of justice due to mistake or violent prejudice, unjust executions may take place; everyone can recall instances; but they are exceptional, and they attract universal attention. Most of the criminals eliminated by death are clearly the enemies of society, and need to be eliminated. I would myself much prefer to see methods of elimination adopted which dispense with the death penalty. The best method, no doubt, is to render the criminal a harmless member of society. By dismissing the question of his death, the criminal ceases to become a sensational object of unwholesome vulgar curiosity, while the possibility of repairing a mistake is preserved. We have been slowly moving towards that end for a century past. So I do not regard the question of capital punishment as any longer urgent.

It is quite another matter when we turn to war. Here

again, I am not concerned with the alleged 'sacredness' of life. Death, like life, one cannot too often repeat, is in Man's hands. There is much to be said for the adoption, under duly regulated conditions, of abortion, infanticide, and euthanasia; Man has accepted them in the past and may accept them again in the future, should they seem desirable. There is much to be said about that, and if this were the occasion I should be prepared to say it. Let us grant that we are free to kill. The question remains: Is war the best way of killing?

Now if I were a reasonable being addressing reasonable beings, I should have no doubt about the answer. Indeed I should hardly trouble to ask the question. A reasonable creature is also humane — for it is reasonable to be true to one's own species — and could not hesitate over the answer. In the special forms to which it has been magnified in our advanced times war is the very worst method of killing. It has ceased to evoke any virtues; it is carried out on a wholesale scale; it destroys men, women, and children; and in so far as it exerts any discrimination it is the best whom it first mangles.

I know of course that we are not reasonable beings. I know that the people whom I address — whether my own fellow-countrymen or in any other properly civilised land — will read what I write and soon afterwards, at the tax-gatherer's command, put their hands meekly in their pockets, just as I do myself, searching painfully for shillings, dollars, or francs in order to pay for a larger army, more battle-ships, heavier bombs, and the latest improvement in poison gas, wherewith on the first favourable opportunity to spread death and destruction on our nearest neighbours. And then, with a smile or a sneer for international tribunals and such-like methods of dealing with national disputes on the basis of justice and humanity, we will eagerly snatch up the paper which describes the amazing details of the latest murder.

So that I scarcely know whether I am not myself an arrant fool to ask these idle questions, and whether I should not do better to appeal to popular sentiment by talking against Capital Punishment.

I only know that the Olympian Gods have always been endowed with an immense capacity for laughter. I can hear them now.

LI

THE QUESTION OF GENIUS
IN WOMEN

IT is quite true, as you have pointed out, that our knowledge does not yet allow of a clear and indisputable conception of "genius." That is inevitable so long as we look at genius as an entity. Lange-Eichbaum goes so far as to say that there is no such thing as a born genius. But Terman in the best study I know, on the experimental comparative basis, of the origin of genius, finds two factors in the childhood of those who later reveal genius, the first a high grade of intelligence, though not necessarily the highest, and the other steadfastness of motive, of which the second is perhaps the most important. It is in this need to be possessed by abstract ideas, or by what I call abstract emotionality, that I seem to see the reason why women have never reached the first rank of genius.'

The writer is a German woman of distinguished ability who has been specially occupied with psychology. It is the conclusion of this passage which interests me here.

Although it may be true, as my friend remarks, that I have not been able to define genius, I have expended much pains-taking interest on its distribution. I have, further, always accepted the conclusion that genius occurs far more frequently among men than among women. That is an instance, as I have sometimes pointed out, of the less range of variation in female traits generally. All sorts of monstrosities and deformities on the physical side are more common in men. It is not surprising that the same should be true of intellectual mutations, and that there should be more genius among men as well as more idiocy. It has never seemed to me that in admitting this conclusion I was departing from the doctrine of sexual equivalence I have always held. Many fallacious and sometimes contradictory arguments have, however, been brought by women against it, so far at least as genius is concerned, for I have not observed that the champions of women have shown much enthusiasm regarding their equality in idiocy. It thus becomes a rare pleasure to find a woman approaching this matter from above, as an intellectual problem, freed from the bondage of sex prejudice.

I was viewing the question from the biological standpoint. So it is interesting to see it approached, and by a woman, from a more psychological viewpoint. My German correspondent, pursuing Terman's argument (though she might also have mentioned Dr. Catherine Cox) into this field, points out that women are not easily capable of exercising an emotionality free from all concrete admixture. Their feelings do not become detached from some person or side-object only loosely connected with any abstract aim. A complete freedom from the concrete is, as my friend at once adds, also extremely rare in men. But now and then it appears, and these men are reckoned in the first rank of genius.

Such men are astonishing to their more ordinary fellow-mortals absorbed in earthly matters. They appear, and sometimes are, so near to insanity, that they seem possessed by some 'demonic' influence.

But women — though a few attain to the second rank of genius and many possess a streak of it — are entrusted with the preservation of the species, and that is an altogether concrete matter. Here are the central interests of women. We come down to the biological foundation of our world. Men are more free to cultivate the intellect. But, so far as Nature's aims are concerned — at all events in our species and in our present stage of development — that is a side-issue, and not always one that is beneficial.

For there are already enough tragic possibilities for women. They need not envy the tragic fate which pursues genius. Let us be content to know that equivalence does not mean identity. The natural equality of men and women is not re-semblance, and, if it were, we should all be the losers. I have been trying to make that clear for many years. I am not hopeful of success.

LII

ART VERSUS SCIENCE

An artist writes to me, as indeed he has written before, about what he feels to be the crushing influence of science in our time. Science, he feels, is victorious over art, and science, as he views it, degrades and vulgarises all it touches.

My friend is a genuine artist as well as an accomplished teacher in the department of arts and crafts of a great city. He carries on the traditions of the English art school of half a century ago when William Morris and Burne Jones and Walter Crane sought, not without success, to withstand what was evil in the Industrial Revolution and to revive the medieval tradition of beauty and use as natural partners.

That Pre-Raphaelite movement in its first form is out of fashion today, and I can sympathise with my friend's sad feelings. Yet I do not for a moment share his attitude.

If there were any real hostility between art and science I should certainly feel alarmed over the fate of art. Science was undoubtedly, though not indeed the motive source of the Industrial Revolution which was economic, a most essential part of the movement. But the sordid trail of ugliness, which in its swift early progress that Revolution everywhere left behind it, was not the outcome of science; it might more truly be described as due to a lack of science.

Today, without doubt, art or no art, the life of our human world is moving along channels of science. From the scientific side we see no hostility to art, but merely an absorption in its own aims. Yet, rightly understood, those aims are not opposed to art, but even involve it. Science has indeed been defined by one of its distinguished votaries as meaning 'knowledge reduced to method.' But 'method' is nothing but art; it is simply that organised order and harmony which are the foundation and essence of all art. To say that science is reducible to method is really to admit that science is ultimately art.

It is enough to think of one of the four major sciences, chemistry — the others being mathematics, physics, and biology — and the place it occupies. Chemistry has always been behind the whole scene of life; we are ourselves in our own bodies marvellous instruments of a chemical synthesis; we are indeed, in a sense, as it has been said, the unconscious beneficiaries or the victims of the chemical correlations of our endocrine organs. Today the process is becoming conscious and active. The chemist is finding his home in countless industries. A single firm is now sometimes engaged in the production of some four thousand different fine chemical products. Among such preparations are today the hormones to which in ourselves personality is largely due. The field is so intellectually attractive, so full of new possibilities, that it has become foolish to attempt to belittle its magnitude or its fascination. The chemist has indeed taken on the task of Nature itself. He is largely engaged in the task of carrying forward natural substances which have run down into quiescent and inactive forms, and bringing them into shapes in which they are active and apt for mingling in the stream of life. He has become, even perhaps without knowing it, a creative artist.

Yet that outlook is not really new. The alliance of art

and science is old. The men of my friend's craft were in early days, within the then limited field of that science, chemists. It was only so that the Van Eycks (if there were really two of them) could have produced those works of art which are still so sound and so brilliant.

So that there is as little occasion for the artist to cry out against science as for the scientist to defame art. When we penetrate beneath the surface of science we find art. We find science when we penetrate the substance of art.

LIII

THE PLACE OF ART IN LIFE

I RAGE when I read of the restraints placed on the spread of genuine knowledge whilst pornography is allowed to flourish. For all his motor cars, railways, airplanes, submarines and high explosives, wireless and television, man's intellect still lags behind his material progress. He is still under the domination of his ancestors, and Nietzsche's saying is still as true today as ever it was: "The living are ruled by the dead!" '

I am quoting from a long letter by a man who works in a coal-mine in South Wales. His letters and his history are always of interest to me. When in youth he first began life as a miner he was beset by melancholy. He could see no reason for life; everything seemed meaningless, and human efforts below ground as full of sound and fury signifying nothing as those on the surface. It was only by gradual steps that he found a central sun around which the universe of his being, as he puts it, might revolve. In this he was aided by eager intellectual tastes; he is a great reader, better able than most to grasp the spirit of what he reads, and of the writers who mark the stages of his spiritual progress I need only name Darwin, Buckle, Schopenhauer, and Nietzsche.

When I read the appreciative letters I receive from this man I derive some consolation. The people who dwell on the surface of the earth often seem to make the pioneering thinker feel that he is but as one of the innumerable winds that blow, not worthy of serious attention, at the most what the prophet Ezekiel grieved that he was regarded, 'a very lovely song of one that hath a pleasant voice and can play well on an instrument, for they hear my words but they do them not.' But my friend the coal-miner's spirit is of another stuff and he knows how (after the fashion of the old-time miner) to hew it into shape by the light of the best illumination that reaches him.

That, however, was not what I set out to say. The passage I quoted seemed to me interesting because it puts from another angle exactly what the artist I brought forward on another occasion had set down from his angle. Man's science is out of relation to Man's art. We have mastered the powers of Nature; we can employ physical forces on the vastest or the most delicate scale according to our desire. But over our own souls and our own lives we have, by comparison, no mastery at all.

We do not know, both my correspondents seem to say, how to make the daily accompaniments and instruments of our life and employment reasonably beautiful and pleasant to our senses. We do not, which is more important, know, except through some heroic discipline, how to bring harmony and happiness into our own souls. We do not even know how to distribute the immense wealth which by our new powers we know how to produce. So that those who need that natural wealth and those who can in abundance produce it gaze at each other helplessly, and both alike starve. Between the human control of Nature and the human art of living there is an immense abyss. In our science we are as the angels; in the art of living we are far outdone by the savages of the Pacific, I mean before our civilisation found them out.

Yet in this sympathy between two men in all respects so widely apart as the artist who engraves on wood and the artist who works in coal I find ground for hope. They are not, either of them, men so very far exalted above their fellows, though one belongs to what we look upon as the select class of artists, and the other to the great army of what it is the fashion to call the proletariat. They both lead fairly ordinary lives in touch with their ordinary fellow-mortals.

Is it too much to anticipate that those ordinary fellow-mortals will also some day be of the same mind, and all move together towards the same human goal?

LIV

WOMAN'S STRUGGLE WITH PASSION

W HY are you so overwhelmingly nice in my direction
— it quite puzzles me!'

I am not conscious of the overwhelming niceness.
I am merely concerned about my little friend, who has on
various occasions written me extremely long letters regarding her personal problems in life. She illustrates a
condition which I have seen revealed, at one time or another, by many of the women of ability I have known —
I am almost tempted to say all of them. Men struggle with
passion, and yet preserve their individuality, and overcome
their passion. Their passions are so often obviously tem-
pestuous, but, on that very account, they are more rapidly
exhausted and the storm is succeeded by calm.

In women the struggle may seem less evident on the surface, but below the surface it is more destructive, from the
very effort at concealment. Perhaps one day the woman
suddenly sees what seems the only solution, and there is an
inquest. It happened, for instance, a few days ago in
London.

A young Austrian woman was in love with a married
Englishman who was in love with her. She came over from
Vienna in response to his passionate appeal. But when she
arrived, her lover had already decided — as I have just
been saying a man does decide — that it would be better
to stay with his wife and family. So the Austrian girl must
set out for home again. But, unlike her lover — and this

again is typical — she had not decided that it was better, and even before the boat-train had started she was found lying on the floor, and beside her the automatic pistol she had succeeded in obtaining. In court the reformed lover admitted it was 'the most brutal thing he had ever done in his life.' The coroner accepted the situation as clear: 'There is no doubt about it, the pistol was to end her life because she found her lover no longer wanted her.' It was evidently all in the natural order of things.

Of course such cases are exceptional. For the most part, when love comes to disturb the course of a girl's life, she accepts it, flinging carelessly aside the career on which before she had set her heart as a path in life. The Austrian was prepared to do so at any cost to herself and others. No doubt my friend, though at a less cost, would also do so.

By one of those coincidences I am always meeting, there reaches me since I wrote my first paragraph a letter from a friend in America which could not be more apt to my point. She has a cousin, a young girl, who with her aid and support has been studying, with all a young girl's eager enthusiasm, for the career of a dancer. Now my friend writes: 'I have been wanting to tell you about the readjustment I have had to go through since Ivy's beau appeared upon the scene. The result is a complete lack of interest in everything she has been taught of dancing. It was as if she had forgotten even the meaning of the word. In spite of my disappointment I hoped that the creative example of others might stir her lagging ambitions. But now I resign myself to the fact that there were not any.'

When my friend speaks of 'creative example' she may well have had Pavlova in mind. I have just been reading with delight John Gill's *The Flight of the Swan*, which seems to me perhaps the best book ever written about a dancer. Pavlova represented the splendid exception to the tendency I have here in mind. For the most part the man (however 'brutal' he may feel himself to be) can subordinate passion to his career. The woman, on the contrary, for the most part turns away from the career, however entrancing it may before have seemed, and accepts the alternative of domesticity or despair. For our masculine mind this seems to be the natural order of things.

I suspect that this also is the reason why the masculine critic still tends to belittle the genius of George Sand. That genius, apart from its fine and varied achievement in the sphere of art, was conspicuously shown in life. Here was a woman who knew how to combine the masculine dominance over passion with the feminine conquest of happy domesticity. We cannot stomach that.

LV

SPINOZA

THIS morning I open a packet and find a new book inscribed to me 'With intellectual salutations.' The author is Benjamin de Casseres, a critic who has known how to win the approval of fine judges outside as well as inside his own country. The subject is *Spinoza*.

Now it so chances that, scarcely half an hour before I opened that packet, the subject of my thoughts had been, precisely, Spinoza. I had even wondered if I had an excuse for writing about that subject. Thus the book arrived at what Bismarck was accustomed to term the 'psychological moment.'

There was nothing, I hasten to add, really marvellous in the conjunction of the two events. I was thinking about Spinoza because yesterday was the tercentenary of his birth and today the papers record the meetings held in Amsterdam and London and elsewhere to celebrate that event. It was certainly by a prevision of the event that Benjamin de Casseres set out to write this book for publication as nearly as possible on the anniversary. He has a claim to write about Spinoza — whom in his sub-title he terms 'Liberator of God and Man' — because he is himself of the family and a direct descendant of the philosopher's sister. He has produced what may well be the most eloquent rhapsody ever sung around Spinoza.

Strange, when one comes to think of it, how often Spinoza, in thought and in life the most quintessential of philosophers, has appealed to those who might be supposed to have little or no interest in pure philosophy.

For myself, I well recall how at the age of twenty, without any preliminary training, I was somehow moved to purchase the complete works of Spinoza in the original Latin, three volumes. My knowledge of philosophy and of Latin enabled me to read the books in only a fragmentary and laborious way, but I found the task fascinating, though at an early stage my friend Howard Hinton, James Hinton's son, borrowed the chief volume, the *Ethica*, and never returned it. He is dead now and no marvellous coincidence is likely to bring that volume back again to my set.

A little later I found that Olive Schreiner not long after publishing her *African Farm*, and as little equipped for philosophy as I, was affectionately hugging Pollock's *Spinoza*, perhaps the best exposition of the subject there is, and eagerly talking about it.

Then I found that Goethe, who at a first glance at his work had seemed so absorbed in the emotional aspects of concrete things, had yet owed to Spinoza a kind of spiritual and intellectual conversion. One might continue the tale. Today Einstein, the greatest of modern scientists, finds in Spinoza 'the greatest of modern philosophers.' He receives the tribute of the most accomplished professional philosophers, and yet he appeals to those who are not philosophers at all at the moments when they are distracted by the need to wring some answer from the Universe.

When one looks a little deeply into Spinoza, one sees why this is so. It is not merely because of that fascinating human perfection to which the man so nearly approached in his life. In his thought also he harmonised the discords that rend us asunder. He combined the rationalist attitude with the religious attitude and put them both on a basis of realism. He achieved a cosmic unity in which a liberated humanity, discarding individual aggressiveness, co-operated in the active vision of things as a whole. There resulted a union of science and mysticism, in a serene and exalted ecstasy disguised in a geometrical shape. It is a cardinal point in this vision that only by following science wherever it leads is any God conceivable. That is why Spinoza was excommunicated by the Jewish Synagogue, condemned as an atheist by fellow thinkers, and so generally ostracised that for a century scarcely anyone so much as dared to quote his writings. That also is why today he is honoured in all lands, equally supreme as a thinker and as a champion of humanity.

If we take a sufficiently wide and lofty survey of the great philosophers we may perhaps conclude that ultimately there are two who dominate the rest. In the ancient world there was Plato. In the modern world there is Spinoza. And it is Spinoza who mainly concerns us.

LVI

THE CRIMINALS WE DESERVE

I HAVE been reading your book, *The Criminal*, and it has struck me that, while much of it would still be considered revolutionary today, many of the reforms you advocated there have, at least in part, come to pass. Would you care to write about these reforms, and also about those which still have to be made?'

So writes the editor of a popular London newspaper concerning almost my earliest book, written more than forty years ago. I have allowed it to go out of print now because it would need too much revision to bring it up to date. Perhaps indeed I ought never to have written it. I did not belong to the criminal world in any capacity, but the subject had made a sudden appeal to my youthful activities on two sides.

In the first place I was fascinated by the new scientific study of criminal anthropology, of which Lombroso was the eager and adventurous pioneer; he is belittled today by those who only recall his mistakes. He furnished an immense stimulus to criminology which persists still, along whatever new lines.

In the second place there was my youthful ardour for social reform, awaking to the fact that the prevailing methods of dealing with criminals were equally unjust and ineffective, both as regards the criminal himself and the society he victimised.

In a remarkably short space of time (which astonishes me

now) I had mastered what was to be known of the new criminology. Aided here and there by a few experts, I produced what could claim to be a clear presentation alike of the existing facts and of the direction of future progress.

My position was that the whole aim of criminology hitherto had been to treat crime as an abstraction and to meet it in an equally abstract way by punishments and prison detentions, framed to fit the degree of the crime but without relation to the criminal who did the deed, or any consideration for a remedial effect upon his special temperament. There were many to admit that this method was hopelessly bad, but few to urge any radical transformation of it.

I argued that what society is up against is not an abstraction called 'crime' but certain individuals who are antisocial simply because they are often ill-born and always ill-bred, and can generally be found on careful examination to be unlike ordinary members of society. That is why they are not amenable to the same motives, so that it is idle to treat them as if they were. The prison may be beneficial for the ordinary citizen and entirely harmless for the admirable persons who for political or similar reasons occasionally occupy it. But the prison is totally unfitted for criminals. What they need is not a cell for philosophic meditation, but an active treatment directed to the cure of defects which vary in each individual and can only be discovered after careful expert investigation. That is to say that what is needed is not a prison but what has been termed a 'moral hospital.' And, as in hospitals for sick bodies, the period of detention for sick souls cannot be fixed beforehand by judges completely ignorant of the delinquent before them, but must be indeterminate. The claims of humanity thus become one with the just claims of society for protection from the injuries inflicted by those who have not yet learnt what they owe to society.

When I look back from the viewpoint of today, I am impressed by the extent to which this conception of the problem of criminality has proved acceptable. Everywhere we find the tendency to regard criminality as a problem for individualisation, and to substitute remedial treatment for a merely abstract system of punishment. I need only mention the Juvenile Psychopathic Institute in connection with the Court at Chicago, which was set up some twenty years ago with Dr. William Healy as Director, and the Institute for Scientific Treatment of Delinquency just now being organised in London.

The insight gained by psychotherapeutic experience in recent times, and notably psycho-analysis, though not the only method of approach, has stimulated this movement. Yet we are still only at the beginning. We still look timidly on any attempt to carry out our aims thoroughly.

It is true that some are content to keep on the old road. Thus Mr. Henry Rhodes has recently pleaded for criminals as a social asset. They keep us alert and watchful, he declares, keyed up for emergencies: 'Perhaps our criminals are necessary.'

That is far too narrow a view. The injury inflicted on society by the anti-social, not only directly but by indirect ways which limit our freedom, far outweighs any benefit they confer. Moreover, it ought to be only too clear that in our civilisation we have ample occasion for alertness and are in no need of the criminal as a social saviour. When, too, we discover that, for the most part, criminals are the direct outcome of defective parentage and bad homes, the civilisation which relied on this sort of salvation would indeed be in a poor way.

It is hopeless to attempt to regard criminality as a blessing. And unfortunately there is no escape from the wise saying of Lacassagne half a century ago: 'Every society has the criminals it deserves.'

LVII

THE PHASE OF DISILLUSION

Democracy as a whole appears to be bankrupt. It is not even depressed, only empty and dumb. The pioneering and revolutionary spirit which marked America of old is at present absent. Gone are the men for whom Whitman and Thoreau spoke. The modern American clamours for slave-labour. The torch of the Liberty Statue should be changed into a whip.'

It is an eager and ardent young American who is writing, the child of the New York of today, which he finds immensely fascinating, 'perhaps the most fascinating human spectacle in all history,' as he once wrote to me. I wonder if he is also the child of today in his estimate of democracy. I do not myself offer an opinion, for I suppose that I am the child of the Whitman and Thoreau tradition which my young correspondent assures me is extinct.

Yet the problem interests me intensely. And since it is also a problem which concerns the generation now reaching political power, I may perhaps be forgiven for returning to it again and again. To so large a problem there is always a new angle of approach.

It is the widespread extent of this rebellion against democracy which makes it significant. Such a reaction might indeed be expected in the New World, where democracy has been carried so far. But we find it equally marked in the Old World, where the relics of earlier systems are still visible and might be thought by some to serve as warnings.

It seems possible, indeed, to accept the generalisation of a popular English essayist who writes only this week: 'It is easier to believe in democracy before it arrives.' But it is in Spain, still with the first bloom of a new Republic, that I find in the outlook of Ortega y Gasset perhaps the most penetrating vision of the place of revolutions in history, and indirectly of the place of democracy in such upheavals.

Societies, when they reach the stage at which we can begin to study them, are, as Ortega points out, based on traditions. But in every society, ancient and modern, comes the time when men break away from traditions and find in themselves the standard of truth. That is the age of reason and logic, the age which subordinates life to ideas. In our civilisation, its pioneer was Descartes in the seventeenth century. But the age of reason, as Ortega acutely argues, is also the age of revolutions and the age of democracy. That is so because the rule of reason means that life can be moulded afresh by one violent stroke in accordance with a system of ideas. That is why the partisans of revolutions, as we see today, are prone to speak of 'ideologies.' Life for them has no inherent force of its own, it is merely something that can be fitted into an 'ideology.'

At this point, no doubt, the Russian Revolution will come to mind. Ortega has little to say of it except to point out that it is another instance of utopian rationalism, based on an abstraction which has no existence in real life, the Marxian 'pure worker.' One can understand why it is that devotees of the Soviet are infuriated by the wide philosophic outlook of Ortega which they completely misunderstand. Indeed many of us are apt to forget that the Russian Revolution does not really belong to our time; it embodies and pushes to extreme many of our ideas, but its systematic utopianism is due to the backwardness of Russian civilisation; it has been born out of due time, the product of a generation which has not yet learnt that, as was said of old of the Sabbath, ideas are made for man, and not man for ideas. The stream of life cannot be poured into an 'ideology.'

If revolutions are out of date, in what phase are we now? Ortega would say one of disillusion. Hope burns low; muscles grow flaccid; vision is narrowed down to personal or at most national aims. Man is not in the mood to face the task of organising the world. On the contrary he acquires the mentality of the slave, the spirit of a dog in search of a master. 'Anything rather than the terror of facing in one's own person the assault of existence!'

Indeed when I read Ortega on this point I realise the significance of the passage I have quoted from my correspondent's letter. The philosopher who views the world from above in Madrid is at one with the youth who mixes with men in New York.

Shall we therefore accept reaction and despair? Ortega bravely denies that any such thing as reaction ever existed. What we so call is merely a 'transitory interval,' the necessary result of revolution.

So let us hold fast to the motto which embodies the faith of the men of Ortega's race who dared to discover America: 'There is more beyond!'

LVIII

THE GOSPEL OF NUDISM

I AM struck by the fact that, despite so much nudism and sun-bathing, many adepts of these cults, often quite young ones, seem lost when the sun deserts them. There is Stella, of course, always mourning for the sun, but in a less degree her type is fairly frequent. Some people spend ridiculously long and I should have thought precious hours in this ritual of nudism, living practically naked all day, getting as brown as berries — and sometimes almost as wrinkled — yet thereby storing up no stamina and gusto to face the cold and wind and rain, as I could in youth. Am I wrong?'

Of recent times many letters reach me, both from England and America, in which this subject of sun-bathing and nudism is touched. The appeals come to me, I suppose, because, more than twenty years ago, in my book on *Sex in Relation to Society*, I had a chapter on nakedness. It was chiefly in regard to education that I discussed the matter, and though I knew that I had behind me the opinion of distinguished educationists I felt it needed courage to come forward in this cause. I was really much more a voice crying in the wilderness than I admitted when I argued that nakedness should no longer be allowed to remain 'the perquisite of those who lust for the obscene.'

Indeed, even many years later, when Dr. Maurice Parmelee wished to publish in the United States his most serious and comprehensive philosophic work on nudism in modern life, he was advised in high quarters that it might be dangerous to do so, and publication in the United States was in fact held back for several years. Today such an attitude seems merely ridiculous. Officialdom, it is true, retains its usual shape, hidebound by traditions of an age that is past. Nudity seeks in vain for the sympathy of the magistrate or the policeman. But among the educated class, as we know, and now indeed in all civilised lands, it is accepted as at all events an attainable ideal under certain conditions. The question that remains is simply as to what are these conditions. The people who raise the question, as I am still sometimes astonished to find, are of the most various sorts. I have, I fear, been almost inclined to ask myself whether nudism, like democracy, is not easier to believe in before it arrives.

My own criticisms of some forms of this movement today are mainly two. In the first place, I endorse the qualifying comment of the friend whose letter I quoted at the outset: the tendency to excess. So many people, as usual, must run to an extreme. The horror of nakedness gives place to a horror of clothing, instead of the realisation that each is good in its time and place. Even on the physical side we not only need the sun, but we need protection from the sun, and Nature has taken care to provide tropical men with ample pigment for that purpose. Violet-ray therapy which, not long since, seemed, in its natural and artificial forms, almost a panacea, is still recognised as valuable, but with precautions and limitations. As for the physical, so also for the spiritual aspects of nudism. To make it an aim in life is both absurd and unwholesome.

My second criticism really hangs on the first. If there is

no reason for making nudism a leading aim in life, why have Societies for its promotion? To me, personally, indeed, the idea of such Societies is odious. I realise the freedom of sun and air by oneself or in common with intimate friends as an occasional gracious and wholesome accompaniment of living. I have no desire to set off for the 'perfectly screened' enclosure where I shall mix indiscriminately with naked strangers for whom I have no personal regard. I recognise that there are many who feel otherwise and have no other opportunity to express their feelings. But I doubt whether any sectarian movement of this kind will do much to transform the world.

That such a transformation is in progress seems, however, fairly clear. In America a distinguished psychologist, Professor Knight Dunlap, believes that in a few years women at all events will show their bodies in public without causing any commotion, while in England another Professor, Dr. Flügel, is of the same mind, and finds that dress may be, after all, 'but an episode in the history of humanity.' These academic views seem, indeed, extreme. I would be content with the age foreseen more than half a century ago by James Hinton when he wrote of the human body: 'It is good you see it. Come to it as you come to daily bread, or pure air, or the cleansing bath.'

Certainly there are the powerful textile interests to be encountered. These we must leave to the conciliatory efforts of such bodies as the American Association of Pools and Beaches who, as some of their recent decisions show, are perhaps even too willing to compromise.

The foregoing called out a letter from the former correspondent who had submitted to me the principles of his gospel of Naturalism (see p. 148), so that I have, after all, lived to see his later developments. He has come down from the attempt at establishing an ecclesiastical Paganism to the practical, though indeed related, organisation of the British and Universal Sun-Bathing Nudist Society. I quote from his letter a passage in which he seeks to counter my criticism of such Societies:

'Societies seem to be a necessary evil created by opposing forces; obviously there should be no need to organise for what is a natural birthright, but you will surely agree that man's rights throughout the ages have been secured by organisation. It is true that individuals and friends can, and I know of instances where they do, find private opportunities, but I also find those people anxious to link up with others, and that is one definite purpose of such Societies. Anything human is imperfect because each individual has one or many imperfections, so that eventually internal troubles are to be expected, and good legislation — if one may use such a strong term — is necessary to counteract these as far as human forethought is capable.

'It may seem inconsistent to agree with you that nakedness should not be dignified with the name of "Cult." The fact is that nudists, with their "back-to-nature" principles, have still a tendency to compromise with conventionalists. Compromise seems to be so deeply attached to human life that it is not surprising if it is about the last thread to be broken. True, it is responsible for untold hypocrisy and deceit with consequent mental and physical misery, but we have to travel some distance yet before that will be generally recognised. To illustrate: nudists use, as we are doing now, the term "sun-bathing" and that is misleading to many. Sun-bathing is merely incidental to nudism, and is certainly not one of its cardinal points. For a similar reason nudity itself is not correctly to be described as a cult, which is rather what is behind nudity, the complete restoration of natural living, than nudity itself; therefore, if the matter were accurately described, it would be "nature cult," a term which I think you would find much more acceptable.

'Thus you will see the direction my mind and actions have travelled since submitting to you the "naturalism" scheme as a religion; it is in the method of practical application that my mind has modified the matter, and no alteration (still less sacrifice of principle), has taken place.'

LIX

THE FUNCTION OF MUSIC

I FEAR that speculations as to what the music they play means are quite over the heads of performing musicians. They take no intellectual interest in music. Their business is simply to play it.'

So writes an occasional correspondent who has always been in close touch with musicians and is himself keenly musical. I do not question that he is right. But one who is not a musician, and yet finds music one of the chief joys of life, is not content to leave the question there.

An English musical critic has lately discussed the distinction between what Vernon Lee terms the 'hearers' of music and the 'listeners'; the terms are rather arbitrarily defined, but by 'hearers' are meant those who lean back passively and allow waves of pleasant sound to flow over them, and if it has a ready-made name and label, then no responsibility rests on them to determinate what it means. On the other hand is the class of 'listeners,' those who sit up to music, spiritually if not physically; they are intent to get to the core of it, to find in it a meaning and a character, which may indeed for many be far from the precise and technical ideas received by trained musicians, but are equally far from the vague emotional waves of sound which submerge those who lie back.

It is to this class of 'listeners,' as I define them (rather differently from Vernon Lee), that I feel myself related, and my attitude evoked the remark quoted from my correspondent's letter. I was explaining my deep distaste for all music composed to a programme.

The music which is written as an accompaniment to words or a story — of which operatic music is the type — stands apart. It deliberately subordinates itself to another art (Wagner's musical dramas, it is admitted, standing in a class by themselves). It exists to heighten and intensify the effects of definite situations and particular words. It is fulfilling a legitimate function of music.

But not the highest function. That is clearly shown by the fact that it abandons its own self-sufficiency to submit to external guidance. Music that is exercising its highest functions relies upon its own power as music. By trying to claim an additional and foreign interest, as illustrating a story or a situation, it ceases to be true to itself.

A quartet composed after a quarrel with an old friend had been made up; a concerto on the composer's wooing and marriage; a symphony on the death of his favourite daughter; a sonata written after a violent attack of diarrhoea relieved by a large dose of chlorodyne — I can quite believe that these occasions and the like may inspire noble and pathetic music. But I do not need to know the nature of the original impulse which became musically sublimated in magnificent forms of art.

There is more than that. Such knowledge is not merely a matter of indifference. These programmes are a positive hindrance; they distract my attention from the music; they concentrate it on the trivial task of guessing at the details of the story illustrated. It may be pardonable to give a symphonic piece a vague name which will mean little or nothing to the listener — such as the 'Tapiola' or

'En Saga' of Sibelius — but anything more than that is a nuisance. It can only bear witness to the composer's ingenuity, not to his mastery of the genuine resources of music.

It is in its transcendency that the peculiar power of music resides. That is to say that music can reach a height on which the accidents of life have ceased to exist. The movement of life subsists, even in a supreme degree, but it is unbound from the limitations of life. Helmholtz said — perhaps in too unqualified a way — that the same music can express either love or worship, and we know that a dance can be converted into a hymn tune. It is because of music's transcendency that we can absorb ourselves in its exploration and even find in it, if we will, the enlarging and consoling expression of all our own varying emotions.

It is a process which may change, but it grows no less as one grows older oneself. A violin, it has been said — though not now with exact truth — is the scraping of the tail of a horse on the bowels of a cat. When as a boy I first heard some famous violinist, whose name I now forget, it sounded something like that. It is a very different matter now when I hear Kreisler or another playing the Violin Concerto of Beethoven or of Brahms.

LX

THE PLACE OF VIOLENCE IN NATURE

THE perfection of good sense, and the objectivity, in your treatment of marriage, as well as the highly human attitude, are admirable. But, for my own part, I have to shift my position to appreciate them. What I see in love is the most violent expression possible of that metaphysical contrariety which is at the heart of existence, and is manifested in jealousy. In creating the sexes, Nature seems to have sought to perpetuate life on the basis of contrariety. The mutual attraction of the unlike opposite sexes is associated with hatred within the like sex, of the male for the male and the female for the female. It remains true that, to render social life possible, the contrariety, which maintains life above the level of identity which would annihilate it, must be reduced to a point at which it no longer involves a struggle to the death; and all your work has been a remarkable contribution to that task.'

I quote (by translating) this rather long passage, not to throw light on my own attitude but because it illustrates the attitude of the writer, who is Jules de Gaultier, by some considered one of the most significant thinkers of our day. This question of violence in Nature generally, and human life in particular, has sometimes aroused mild dispute in our correspondence, for while I accept conflict and the play of opposing forces in Nature and in life, I do not admit that they necessarily involve violence. Therefore I am pleased to note here what seems some approximation to my own outlook.

The place of violence in our universe — I have said it before but I am constantly reminded of the necessity to say it again — has been vastly over-estimated. Undoubtedly it has a place, and the people who crave for a namby-pamby goody-goody world will never be happy in our universe. It is an inescapable fact that violence from time to time emerges in Nature. It takes the form of catastrophe. But Man is so made that it is possible for him largely to safeguard life against catastrophe and to play a brilliant part by Nature's side (or God's if you will) in the constructive work of the world.

Certainly for primitive Man — of whom there are still many representatives among us — and even for science until recent times, violence in Nature seemed normal. The universe itself was thought to have been created with incredible violence in a few days, and geology until a century ago was based on catastrophal theories.

Thus it has happened that our progress in sound thinking has constantly meant putting violence in its place, no longer as the typically natural operation but as abnormal, destructive, in a sense unnatural, because it disturbs rather than furthers the natural order. The earthquake and the active volcano reveal violence in Nature, but the more violent the more exceptional. Two distinguished scientists of Oklahoma, as we know, have lately found reason to believe that nearly two hundred thousand square miles of the earth's surface were once devastated by collision with a giant comet. But that may only happen once in a million years.

It is not otherwise in the living world. Violence may occur. In human society, as we know it, there are revolutions, there are wars; there have been devastating plagues and epidemics. These we have sought to master, mostly with success. We still illogically tolerate revolutions and wars. Yet they are abnormal, destructive, in a sense, unnatural. Revolutions achieve good results, if even any, in so painful and disorderly a fashion that they merely illustrate the ancient tag that the more haste the less speed. Wars may have been noble and beneficial exercises in the days of Homer, though exceptional even then, or it would not have been necessary to write an immortal poem over a struggle which took place so long before its blind poet lived. But war has now entirely changed in character; it is emphatically not idealism, discipline, courage, comradeship, as a prominent thinker of today has truly said, but torture and murder and rapine and rape and falsehood and imposture. When a former British Prime Minister recently remarked in the House of Commons in a matter-of-fact way that fighting ('fighting for safety' as he rather disingenuously termed it) was, with reproduction, one of the two natural instincts which make for the preservation of the species, and 'the oldest instinct we have in our nature,' the statement was not only incorrect as regards the past but flagrantly antiquated and absurd as regards the present. Yet it was meekly accepted by his hearers without one dissenting voice.

It is clear that the devotees of the old catastrophic theory of Nature still survive numerously among us. Let us hope that when the next giant comet is due they may all happily gather together to greet that verification of their theories, and die thankfully. We who survive need not be unthankful.

LXI

THE EXPLANATION OF CRIMINALITY

A CORRESPONDENT who, though an active business man, interests himself in the treatment of young criminals, wishes that I would call further attention to the matter. He finds that, in spite of the general increase in humane methods, there is still too often, at all events in England, a harshness exercised which amounts to cruelty. He points out that when the British Government a year ago, with the general support of the House of Commons, proposed to abolish the decaying punishment of birching for young offenders, the House of Lords insisted on its retention, since when the practice seems to have been revived, even in the hands of women magistrates.

It has to be admitted that, in a highly conservative and traditionalised land like England, the Biblical method of bringing up children with the aid of the rod, though dying out in general practice, is still regarded as the ideal and thus finds its last home on the judicial bench. The pioneering activities of the United States in this field have not altogether Americanised England. For my own part I would make all magistrates who are liable to exercise the functions of a Juvenile Court, and especially all women magistrates, first pass an examination in such a book as the *Youth in Conflict* of Dr. Miriam van Waters, not only a wise and beautiful book but soundly practical. They would learn much there which they could not learn down in that land of the East where, as another wise American long since remarked, 'they did not know everything.'

Yet the problem of youthful delinquency remains, in America as elsewhere, even when we have lightly thrown aside the Biblical rod and the ancient doctrine of punishment, the 'eye for an eye' of the *lex talionis*. A few years ago, if not still, seventy-five per cent of the prisoners in Sing Sing were under twenty-one years of age. In every civilised country crime is found to be a mainly youthful phenomenon. Indeed those who have lived much among criminals have often found, as Dostoevsky found among the convicts in Siberia, that to a large extent they continue children throughout life.

It remains desirable to attribute youthful delinquency, as we are now taught, to 'maladjustment.' But when all allowance is made for the influence of ignorant or foolish parents and an unhappy home environment — undoubtedly it is an important influence — we have not grasped the whole root of the matter.

We are indeed here brought back to the point I have touched on before: the place of violence in human nature. While we always have to beware of overestimating that place, its minor forms remain in Nature, and in human nature they tend to break out in the young, often in ways that are destructive, and in effect cruel. Not long ago, in the neighbourhood of London, a gang of five schoolboys were found amusing themselves by killing and maiming twenty sheep; the boys were sent to an Industrial School; it is quite possible they may turn out estimable men; it is also possible that from time to time they may exhibit, in more disguised forms of patriotism or what not, those traits of callousness and violence which, in the eyes of many, discredit any optimistic estimate of the human race.

It was at one time thought that criminality might be largely accounted for by defective intelligence; criminals are weak-minded and on this ground outside normal humanity. So in some respect a considerable proportion undoubtedly appears to be. But it is a mistake, as Professor Carl Murchison of Clark University showed in a masterly study, to suppose that, when submitted to the ordinary mental tests, criminal intelligence is always inferior; it is even possible to regard it as superior to the average. We have to look deeper in organic temperament. As Willemse (working along the lines opened out by the genius of Kretschmer) has found in South Africa, we may find clues to delinquency in constitutional type. Not everyone is born with the constitution that lends itself to crime, yet that tendency is rooted in human nature.

It still remains true that by our bad conditions we may develop the tendency into monstrous forms or by our sound social hygiene control and subdue it. So we may recognise the balance of heredity and environment.

We cannot indeed usually expect the same people to see both scales of the balance. When the sanguine educationist Sulzer expatiated to Frederick the Great on the native goodness of mankind and the need for less harshness in schools, 'Oh, my dear Sulzer,' interrupted the King, 'you don't know the damned race as I do!'

LXII

SEX AND LOVE

ORIENTALS seem to concern their thoughts far less with sex than we Westerners do... and I often wonder if they can love as we do. The Easterner generally regards woman either as the mother of sons or as the plaything. Of course the better type of Oriental is a past-master in the art of love.'

It is a young English artist who is writing, a girl who has lived in various parts of the world and is fascinated by the East. As she is not only an artist but a personality, I often find her reflections suggestive. She seems on the present occasion to have indicated a relationship which may be significant.

The relationship I mean is that between what is called 'sex' and what is called 'love.' We sometimes, indeed, tend to look upon these words as meaning much the same thing. But is there not a sense in which they may mean opposite things?

When we take a broad survey of the course of social history, love seems to reach the highest exaltations and refinements of which it is susceptible where sex indulgence is difficult; and as sex freedom increases love seems to diminish. In the classic world of Greece and Rome, which freely accepted sexual indulgence, we find few traces in the literature, until a late period, of what we should call love.

With the coming of Christianity the scene changed. Ascetic ideals prevailed; a heavy hand was placed on sex.

But romantic love began to flower, even in the earliest centuries. Renan long ago dwelt with enthusiasm on 'the infinite joys of chastity' and the exquisite romances of love which the early Church delighted in. Then, later, all the great stories of love, in poetry and in life, began to take shape. The hostility to sex, the existence of a barrier, was always of their essence. The protagonists might even be priests and nuns. But the conception of love grew in magnitude. In Dante it became at last the pivot on which the universe turned. In no shape or form could it have been that in the ancient world.

The Puritan revolution reinforced the ban on sex. But it fortified love. We may note that it specially prevailed in a land and in an age which had glorified women, for England was termed on the Continent 'the Paradise of women.' The reaction in our time against what is often called Victorianism has led some to adopt an easy indulgence in sex. An acute critic of our time (who indeed sometimes seems to me unduly pessimistic), Aldous Huxley, has called attention to the result. They have merely, as he points out, bartered the Puritanic repression of sex for 'the deadening influence of promiscuous indulgence.'

And now I seem to see the same opposition when, overlooking all minor historical fluctuations, we compare generally the West with the East. In the East, also, the facility of sexual indulgence is 'deadening' to love. The technique of sex is not necessarily the art of love and may be antagonistic to it. So my young artist friend, who knows and admires Orientals, may be justified in her instinctive fear that they cannot love as Westerners love.

The Oriental, I am sure, will protest. And from our

own Western literature he may quote the contemptuous remark of George Eliot concerning that 'word of all-work "love," ' and the bitter conclusion of Ibsen that 'no word is so full of falsehood and fraud as the little word "love." '

LXIII

GEORGE MOORE

I SHALL be so pleased if you will come and dine with me on Thursday evening.'

That simple invitation was the substance of almost the only letter I ever received from George Moore. It was long ago, in 1898, but I recall it when now I hear that George Moore died yesterday. It seems a trivial occasion to recall, but the sequel had been characteristic. For on Thursday morning came this note written on Wednesday evening: 'I waited dinner half an hour but you did not come. I suppose you forgot. I thought we could have gone to the meeting together afterward.'

I no longer recall what meeting it was, though I know I hastened to reply that the misunderstanding was not on my part. But therewith the correspondence ended; the invitation, for whatever reason, was never renewed.

My acquaintance with George Moore was, indeed, less a direct relationship than the by-product of his friendships with friends of mine, for a short time with Olive Schreiner and for many years with Arthur Symons. As for a considerable period I shared chambers in the Temple with Symons when Moore was also living in that delectably peaceful place, I would frequently come across him and we would pause for brief conversation.

One occasion I specially recall when, knowing that I took some interest in the matter, he stopped me to talk with deep emotion, in reference to a then recent case, of the fate of young women who are compelled, by the hostile attitude of society, to destroy their illegitimate babies. Such tender human sympathy was one of his most pronounced traits, though it may perhaps surprise those who regard him simply as an apostle of art for art's sake.

Certainly Moore's ideal was that of the pure artist. Nor has any writer in English of our time, and seldom of any time, laboured so indefatigably throughout a long life to attain to the summit of that ideal. With an early life in Paris and consequent French interests, his first literary god was naturally Flaubert, and it was a worship with which I could sympathise. I recall how once, in Olive Schreiner's little sitting-room I sat between Moore and Karl Marx's daughter, Eleanor, who had just been translating *Madame Bovary*, and how eagerly he sought for her approval of the supreme rank he assigned to *L'Education Sentimentale*.

Later in life, Moore drew away from Flaubert, and French interests generally, in favour of an almost Puritanic cult for English literature and the purity of the English language. A few years ago he wrote to the London *Times* to complain of the usage by me and others of the verb 'intrigue' in the French sense, but, as I pointed out to him, I was prepared to defend that usage. With this English development came a new worship for Landor in style, a worship which, even to so confirmed a Landorian as I am, seemed rather extravagant, yet was the outcome of a stern and classic ardour.

In real life Moore was a figure hardly displaying the same characteristics. His remarkable features and peculiar expression have often been well reproduced. Yet the best representation of him I have ever seen is offered by some of the cat-mummies, one especially, in the Egyptian department of the British Museum. That extraordinary resemblance has often puzzled me, but there it unmistakeably is.

Moore's human emotions somehow did not suffice to bring him into close relation with life. He was even lacking in respect for the facts of life, save as clay for the artist to mould. So it happened that when he planned to meet Verlaine for the first time, and something prevented the meeting, he was so annoyed (though later a meeting seems to have taken place) that he wrote an account of it, in the manner he felt sure it would have occurred, as an actual occurrence. He here described Verlaine as unbinding and displaying his ulcerated leg, which no one who knew the poet could regard as a likely incident.

I find the same maladjustment to the facts of life in a story which was told me from a reliable source of Moore's visit to the Wagner Festival at Baireuth when he was staying in Munich. After the performance, kind friends carefully indicated to him the Munich train on the Baireuth platform. Half an hour later they were surprised to find him still pacing the platform. 'Well,' he said, in explanation, 'I may be a fool, but I am not such a fool as to get into a train which is going to München when I want to go to Munich.'

That confession was interesting and, as on that occasion, not altogether unfounded. Moore really belonged to a family including not only some members of distinction, but some, I understand, who were eccentric or defective. He might himself have ended life as a failure, if it had not been that, by some exquisite chance of Nature, he was able to base, on that uncertain foundation in life, a supreme achievement in art. He illustrates the relationship of genius I have sometimes pointed out, not, as is sometimes supposed, with insanity, but, however remotely, with imbecility.

In the sphere where we usually apply the title, George Moore was by no means a saint. But he will live as a saint of art.

LXIV

THE AMERICAN ON ENGLAND

I LIKE England very much! I like the English people too, and I didn't expect to, having always heard of them as aloof, humourless, and hypercritical of Americans. Those whom I have met — on the ship and in my flittings among various hotels and pensions — have been, without exception, kind-hearted, hospitable, and excellent company! I think you have been very much maligned.'

The writer is an American woman from the Far West who has never left the States until now when, at the age of thirty-six, she comes direct to England on her first visit abroad.

The opinions which people cherish regarding foreign lands always seem to me full of interest. Not necessarily because they are right or because they are wrong, but because they cannot fail to be significant of personal or national attitudes, which may sometimes indeed be fateful.

How far my friend's estimate of American opinion of the English is correct I do not know. I do not hear it from those Americans who come to England because they prefer that land to America. No doubt, similarly, there are English people who paint a correspondingly unattractive picture of Americans. It is from a country's own children, however, that chastising criticisms are wont to come. Thus in regard to the War Debts question, I have heard that the name of 'Uncle Shylock' is supposed to be applied to the United States by the English. But it was, we learn, really an American who invented the term. How much ill-will may be caused by such misunderstandings!

The New World, notwithstanding, has always been singularly fortunate, with whatever passing clouds, in enjoying the sunshine of the Old World's favours. 'We are heer in Paradice,' wrote an Englishman, John Winthrop (I like to recall he was English since his father chanced to be the neighbour and friend of my family in Groton village), from New England to his wife in Old England nearly three centuries ago. From that day and earlier America has stood for freedom to romantic idealists and for El Dorado to hard-headed realists. Both lures alike have led myriads of European migrants to cast off their old nationalities for a new allegiance. It seems a happy fate.

Very different and more chequered has been the fate of England in the estimation of other peoples. From time to time I recall the fact that a certain Lesuire entitled a book on the English, *The Savages of Europe*. That, indeed, was in the eighteenth century. But a little later, Montalembert, a Frenchman who was partly English, said that no nation has changed less than the English and that modern England is all to be found in germ in the twelfth century. So keen a critic as Taine seems to have been of much the same opinion when he emphasised English stability and said that of all the peoples of Europe the English is the most capable of transforming without recasting itself, a conclusion, I may add, which is sometimes independently put forward by thinkers of today who argue that if England ever becomes a Communistic State, it will not be by the path of revolution.

And then I recall the opinion of John Stuart Mill, English

himself indeed, though often a critic of England, and a lover of France, where at last he died, that, more than any other, the English people is the product of civilisation. The artificiality and formality on the English surface which sometimes repels the stranger would thus be accounted for. But it is all very puzzling for the Englishman who wishes to reform himself. Is he not civilised enough? Or is he too civilised?

It remains puzzling when we turn to consider special aspects of the English people. English women, for instance, have from of old found admiration among the people of various European lands. Half a century ago, the Italian anthropologist, Mantegazza, who knew both the Old World and the New, concluded that at her best the Englishwoman — it was the often abused Victorian Englishwoman — is one of the two highest forms of life (the other being the Andalusian woman) in the human world, and both are divine.

'English women,' writes to me now, on the other hand, a friend who has lived in various countries, and is also, like Mantegazza, a physician, 'English women are the least attractive I have seen anywhere; they are tastelessly dressed, pseudo-masculine in manner, poor in physique, and wanting in charm.' So what are we to believe? Perhaps what Tilly, who knew well both the women of the Old and the New World, concluded: 'Two things must be owned: one is that there are perhaps more beautiful women [not always charming he admits] in England than elsewhere; and the other that when an Englishwoman sets out to be ugly, she goes beyond anything.' But, at all events, there seems justification for those in every country who feel that, whatever foreigners think of them, they themselves know better.

Perhaps, indeed, we may conclude by accepting the recent utterance of a popular English essayist: 'Indifference to the opinion of others is the first step towards wisdom.' Certainly, for many, that seems only a counsel of perfection. First steps, as every infant knows, are difficult.

LXV

KEYSERLING'S 'SOUTH AMERICAN MEDITATIONS'

PLEASE tell me whether you already own my *South American Meditations*. If not I would be glad to present you with it. I think that this book, which I consider to be the most important I ever wrote, should appeal, most of all Anglo-Saxons, to you, for you are the least biassed by Puritan heredity.'

It is Count Keyserling who is writing, and I have now received and read the *Meditations*, whether or not with that freedom from Puritan bias with which the Count endows me. I have certainly observed that some of my friends are wont to credit me not only with freedom from Puritan bias but even with a violent Anti-Puritan bias. I am not conscious of it. I would even say that I have a deep admiration for the Puritan virtues, that is of course in so far as they are real, not mere hollow conventions. I would far rather be accused of exhibiting the heroic vigour and independence of the old Puritans than the flabby weakness and indifference of many modern Anti-Puritans. I might even be willing to claim that I am myself a Puritan, though of a newer and more comprehending brand. In the days of the old English Civil War my forefathers, even when they happened to be of the same family, were active on both sides, and were I myself placed back in that age, I feel that if I were a Cavalier it would be with Falkland, and if I were a Roundhead with Marvell, that is to say, often with one foot in the opposite camp. As it is, I am aware of no bias to overcome in reading Keyserling's *Meditations.*

The Count's almost pathetic anxiety over this book, I also think I can understand. I have heard more or less of the antagonism it has aroused in the United States, the 'tremendous enmity and hatred' as he himself expresses it to me. I have been tempted to remind him that he has perhaps invited it. If he has previously, as I understand, referred to the United States as a big kindergarten it is natural that the inmates should wish to make themselves heard and felt. In the present volume 'Americanisation' seems always to be coupled with 'Bolshevisation' as desouling influences, and while Keyserling expects salvation to come from woman it is not from the 'defeminised and masculinised' North American woman. 'South American sadness,' he thinks, 'is worth more than all North American optimism.'

It is the mark of the prophet to tell what seem to him home-truths with the most innocent, if not reckless, disregard of consequences. That is why prophets have always been in hot water, and sometimes even in hot flames. And Keyserling is of the tribe of the prophets much more than of the philosophers with whom he sought to associate himself.

For anyone brought up on the Bible it is easy to come into touch with Keyserling, however widely different his message may be from that of the prophets of the Hebrews. He has the same impetuous impulse to utter the affirmations of his own soul, the same calm assurance that those affirmations come from the heart of the Universe, the same liability to infuriate the public he is innocently seeking to warn of the wrath to come.

That typical prophet, Jonah, was prepared for his mission of denunciation at Nineveh, then the centre of what our modern prophet would call Americanised civilisation, by a sojourn of three days and nights in the belly of a great fish. For Count Keyserling the whale, as we used to call it, has been South America, and the effect greater even than upon Jonah. It has produced a kind of spiritual revolution with, as its outcome, this his most significant book.

How far that Southern continent may justifiably exert such an influence I cannot decide. My own acquaintance with South America is confined to a few weeks spent in Peru in childhood, and I recall little more than the patios of Lima with the outline of the distant Andes and the ammoniacal odour of the Chincha Islands. But, even from a distance, and perhaps on the foundation of these early impressions, South America in its varied and so often troubled aspects has seemed fascinating; I have liked to believe that, as Keyserling now declares, it can never be 'Americanised,' and that it holds a great promise for the future along other than industrial and commercialised lines.

The interest of these *Meditations*, however, is not chiefly for the possibilities of the lands that inspired them, though there it is suggestive. It is in the reactions of those lands on the highly original and richly cultured personality of the visitor. South America has brought to him a clearer vision of the world in its essence. He is not merely concerned to denounce a mechanised and standardised and narrowly intellectualised civilisation. He now discerns more vividly what stands above that civilisation, lost in its old forms, but still within the reach of future achievement. The 'soul' in its old shapes is out of fashion and suppressed. So far as those old shapes involved superstitions and taboos now outworn, that is well. But we forget that the soul also involved the attainment of joy and gaiety. 'I know of no sour nor bitter saint,' Keyserling declares. For Dante the Universe was made of Hell and Purgatory and Paradise, and the whole constituted a 'Comedy.' In the drab and solemn pedestrian civilisation which we have forged for ourselves we have forgotten that the essence of life for the soul is play, and the world is its theatre. It may be an inevitable phase we are passing through. But there is more beyond.

That is why these *Meditations* are, far more than the passing impressions of a tourist, a treatise, as the sub-title has it, *On Hell and Heaven in the Soul of Man.* It may be profitable to read it together with the record of another journey, the *Voyage au Bout de la Nuit* by the French doctor who calls himself Louis-Ferdinand Céline, a journey through Hell which never reaches Heaven.

But if in spirit, though not in race, of the tribe of the old Hebrew prophets, Keyserling may be safe from one complaint those old prophets were wont to make. Ezekiel bemoaned that the public treated him merely as one that 'hath a pleasant voice and can play well on an instrument.' It may be the translator's doing, but Keyserling cannot raise that complaint.

LXVI

THE PROBLEM OF LEISURE

I HOPE you will not mind receiving a few lines from a working man. I have recently read the three books of your *Impressions and Comments* in our local Central Library, so different in their sanity and common-sense from the blatant rubbish so many choose for their mental food. Working men have so much forced leisure now that many are turning to reading, and to serious reading as our Library figures show. I have worked for thirty-two years in a South London factory employing six hundred people, and the change in their attitude to serious authors during the last two years is perhaps unrealised by those not in touch with workshop life. Many of my mates have entirely discarded newspapers, regarding them as "dope." Politicians of every description are derided. They are turning to *writers*. We collect pennies to buy second-hand cheap editions of books to read during our "suspension weeks." The significant thing is that workers today are looking to authors who have the power to stimulate thought, express ideas and ideals, and focus public opinion.'

I quote from this letter, just received, not to furnish a testimonial (which I trust may not here be required) to my own sanity and common-sense, but because it has much more than a merely personal significance. It touches a problem which a few of us are seriously beginning to ponder. What is to be done about the increased leisure in the world?

At the moment, that is even an acute problem. In all

the larger countries there are today millions of people accustomed to work, even to prolonged and exhausting work, who are now workless. In the Old World where periods of industrial depression are recognised as liable to occur, the situation is met, so far as possible, by organised systems of insurance and doles, which keep the workers just within the limits of subsistence. In the New World, where the level of prosperity has been so high hitherto, it has seemed needless to provide for its absence. But beside that poignant problem, both worlds alike see now arising this of the increase of leisure.

For the working class, in England at all events, there has long been the excitement of sport, various forms of gambling, and the picture house. Passive enjoyments all of them, mentally as well as physically, and therefore — however contemptible they seem to many — the inevitable recreations of a working class actively absorbed in labour. But under the new conditions they are seeming less satisfactory. All sorts of social activities are now being organised to develop physical activity, such as in England the National Council of Social Service, enlisting the help of voluntary bodies to provide for the occupation and recreation of the unemployed and to care for their welfare generally.

At the same time we are beginning to reap the advantages of our national systems of education (my correspondent tells me his parents could scarcely read or write) and of the museums and public libraries we have slowly been building up. The worker, no longer forced to think about his own immediate work, is free to think about larger problems — indeed even forced by the world's situation to think about them — and so he turns to those neglected fountains of knowledge. That is why my correspondent's letter is significant. The factory operatives of today, we find, meet to discuss G. H. D. Cole's *Intelligent Man's Guide through the World Chaos*, and H. G. Wells' *Work, Wealth and Happiness of Mankind*, and for fiction turn to the books of Virginia Woolf.

The problem happens just now to be acute. But it will soon be chronic. We know that never again will constant and exhausting manual labour absorb mankind as during the last century it was absorbed. When in the earlier days of humanity megalithic circles were set up and the Pyramids built the expenditure of human labour was prodigious. Those were the great days of the proletariat. At the beginning of the modern machine age there was a tremendous recrudescence of human labour. But that very demand for labour led to methods of dispensing with it. As we know, the new technical advances are now so rapid that human labour is being reduced to a minimum. We already hear of a four-hours working day as the probable maximum for the future. The day of the proletariat is over. Few workers but skilled ones are now needed. Most of the unemployed of today will never be employed again. They already belong to an age that is past.

That is why the problems of eugenics are now absorbing so much attention. That, to return to the point before us, is why the problem of leisure is acute. The old roads are barred. And therewith mankind sees opening the ascending paths to fresh heights of achievement.

We are brought at the end to a great truth I have often encountered in life. It is on our failures that we base a new and different and better success. Along the road we seemed to find so successful we suddenly encounter a check. It is the stimulus to find another road for which we are perhaps better fitted, and one which may lead us to greater triumphs.

Adam and Eve were driven out of their little Eden. They must have counted themselves sad failures. But they gained the whole world.

LXVII

REBELLION AND RESIGNATION

THIS is a terrible age we are living in and especially bad for the young (I am now twenty-one). The others, having already lived, don't care what happens. It is tragic that the young must inherit a world for which they are not responsible. In these times no one is safe. A day, an hour, may bring about revolutions, national bankruptcies, or assassinations. I pick up a newspaper with dread and fear of some catastrophic change in world conditions. If the oldest governments were to be destroyed tomorrow I would not be surprised. Such is the temper of mind in which we young moderns live.'

I quote a young correspondent in New York from whose letters I have had occasion to quote before. Even since the words were written he might claim that his attitude is more than ever justified.

It may seem justified indeed, not only when the young experience despair or apprehension but even when they seek boldly to face what looks to them like chaos and to re-mould the world nearer to heart's desire. For there are always the old, who when young might have been on their side but have slowly through life dug themselves carefully in against all disturbing influences and now feel nothing but contempt or indignation for those who would disturb their world afresh, even in order to better it.

To take a conspicuous instance: it was not so long ago that a Great War was fought. The main object of that war, it was freely stated on the allied side, was 'to end war' and to annihilate militarism, incidentally also 'to make the world safe for democracy.' That was an aim that appealed to the younger generation; they threw themselves eagerly into the war, even before any pressure was put upon them to do so, and it could not have been fought if they had not done so. The War was brought to a triumphant close, and the defeated side placed under a restraint which, at all events, put a temporary end to their initiative in war.

But that was obviously only part of the task. It remained for the men of the victorious side to proclaim that their object in fighting had been achieved, that for them also war was at an end and to be replaced by more reasonable methods of settling national disputes. Endless impediments have been placed by the stolidly inert forces of established officialdom in the way of the concrete realisation of that object. It was natural that the younger generation should begin again to assert itself.

In England that seems to be happening, and even in Oxford, which has long been regarded as 'the home of lost causes' and the last place from which to view the light of any dawn. But of late there has been a decided movement towards the Left at Oxford, on the part of the more thoughtful undergraduates who concern themselves with the affairs of the world, a movement not necessarily associated with definite parties, cliques, or cranks. Thus they could not fail to realise the fateful nature of the Disarmament Conference now moving with such slow steps toward what might well have seemed the most splendid goal the world at present has in sight.

The best thought of undergraduate Oxford has always been most conspicuously reflected by the Oxford Union, a society with which for generations many of the finest Englishmen have in youth been connected. The Union has lately discussed the question of how the solemn pledge given to the men who fought and died for King and Country between 1914 and 1918, that the war was 'a war to end war,' could best be given effect. After a debate of exceptionally high tone in an unusually large gathering, the motion was carried by a majority of 275 votes to 153, 'That this house will in no circumstances fight for King and Country.'

The resolution had been put into what may seem a youthful provocative form. But so definitely concrete a statement at all events seemed to make clear the opposition between those who wish to carry on the work of reforming the world and those who are content to bring the reform to an end, between, that is to say, the young and the old, though, we must remember, there are always old spirits among the young (153, we see, even in the Oxford Union) and always young spirits among the old. There was a wild outcry among those who seem to know nothing of our traditional English way of dealing with kings. Amid still more vulgar forms of abuse a packet of 275 white feathers arrived (and were, it is said, proudly worn), while the more dignified old people talked about the 'Children's Hour.'

So on the one hand we have the young men, desiring with Ibsen to place a bomb under the arch which supports what seems an effete civilisation and to create it anew. On the other hand are the old, saying (was it once said by Goethe?) 'Thank God I am no longer young in so thoroughly finished a world.' Rebellion and aspiration on one side: thankful resignation, if not contentment, on the other side. The two attitudes seem complementary. They are both needed to make the complete Man. A strange creature, no doubt.

LXVIII

OUR MACHINE AGE

A LONDON editor has asked me to write about the place of the machine in the age we are approaching. That invitation seems to me an interesting sign that an old problem is just now felt to be an actual concern.

It may also be a sign that some need is felt of clear vision on this problem. One does not discern much at present. Even the British Chancellor of the Exchequer, who might be expected to be at the centre when such questions are involved, has just declared that our troubles today are largely due to 'the advances in the invention of labour-saving machinery,' and leaves out completely the question of the social control of those advances. For the more literary and romantic attitude towards machines, we may turn to Mr. Sherwood Anderson. If we look at his memorable *Story-Teller's Story* we see him manifesting for most of his life an attitude of repulsion towards mechanisation as destructive of individuality, and cherishing a longing for the old ideals of craftsmanship, while more recently he has taken the side of the machine, yet with no clear realisation of the problem, first or last.

But that problem has been long enough open for investigation. In England it became acute a century ago and more, when both the forces hostile to machinery were aroused into activity. For there are two forces in our nature, quite different and even opposite, which rebel against the machine: the force of realism and the force of idealism. The practical hard-headed conservative realist is opposed to the invading machine because it upsets his established habits and disturbs his vested interests. The romantic idealist is up against the machine because it breaks in on his own preconceived vision of harmony and beauty in life and nature, as well as destroying arts and crafts that are ancient and venerable.

So at the Industrial Revolution the workers attacked and destroyed the new factories because they thought their means of livelihood were being taken away. And a little later the lovers of Nature and art arose in fury and fulminated against the railways which cut up the loveliest landscapes, and the looms which superseded the most exquisite handicrafts. I could myself have joined in the outcry with special reference to the disappearance from our globe of the sailing ships which I was familiar with in childhood. But I should have been wrong.

The realists and the idealists were both wrong. Both alike — though they never knew it and do not indeed always realise it today — were fighting against Nature.

For, as so often happens, the whole question would have fallen to the ground if only those who worried over it had taken the trouble to ask themselves the question: What is a machine?

In the most elementary sense, as the dictionary helps us to realise, a machine is simply a means, a contrivance for reaching an end which, without it, would less easily be reached. So that, really, the first flint knife and scraper which Man devised in the early Stone Age, to do what previously teeth and nails had less easily done, was a machine. No doubt the realists and idealists of that age were both alike indignant at this new invention which displaced the wholesome and enjoyable methods of old time and brought mechanisation and standardisation into the world.

But there is more than that to be said. The hand itself that wielded the flint knife is a machine, a contrivance developed for effecting movements which the quadruped could with difficulty, or never at all, effect with his paw. And then we realise that our whole bodies are machines, supplied with endless devices such as we constantly employ to act on the external world. We are ourselves natural machines. The romantic idealists and the obstinate realists who set themselves to oppose the machine were fighting against Nature.

'The organised prolongation of ourselves' — that is the definition of the machine which commends itself to the expert investigator. Mechanology, the science of the machine, is thus a kind of biology; machines form serial parallels to living organs, and animal species; they are generated and developed, become degraded and die. The man who sets himself up against machinery can only show his sincerity by suicide.

But then there is this difference between the machines we ourselves are and the machines we create. Over those our control is limited, over these it is absolute. We are free to control these, and free to be controlled by them and become their slaves and even their victims. That is where the enemy of machinery finds his justification. So it is possible for Sherwood Anderson to maintain that mechanisation means standardisation and that standardisation means impotence.

Less than a century ago it was said that 'machinery is a fiend to the poor.' Today I find a popular essayist writing: 'Most of us love machines as the poet of an earlier world loved birds and flowers.' But that charming essayist forgets that the most tremendous machine of today is still the war-machine.

LXIX

THE PROBLEM OF STERILISATION

SOME thirty years ago an American physician, living in Chicago but of Puritan New England ancestry, wrote to tell me of his experiences. He was forty years of age, married, and with several children. Not desiring more, he resolved, as a safe and definite method of contraception, to submit to sterilisation by vasectomy. The operation was simple, not even causing a single day's absence from work, and the results entirely satisfactory both to him and his wife. 'If I shed even the faintest ray of light on this greatest of human problems,' he concluded, 'I shall be glad indeed.'

That pioneering step, as it may fairly be called, was recorded in 1910 in my book *Sex in Relation to Society*. Since that date sterilisation has been widely practiced with success as a method of birth control, and is constantly spreading. Whenever it is undesirable to have more children, or not desirable to have children at all, sterilisation is the best and safest method of birth control. There can be no doubt that it will eventually be so regarded.

True that some simple-minded persons in the past, and even today, have questioned whether sterilisation is legal; and there are lawyers, whose business it is to invent quibbles, still ready to hint that this little operation is a form of the medieval offence of *mayhem*. That in old days was properly an offence, for it meant the violent deprivation of a limb useful for defence in fighting. But the operation of vasectomy no more affects self-defence than the operation of shaving, and it is not usually thought that we need legalise the razor.

We cannot take these quibblers seriously. The country that allowed them to abolish by legislation the citizen's right to limit his own procreative activities would have lost every spark of manly self-respect.

Thus we are led to the aspect of the matter now to the front: the question of eugenic sterilisation. If it is reasonable to regard sterilisation as a permissible contraceptive when offspring are no longer desired, it is equally reasonable to regard it as imperative when there is a possibility — if not a probability — that the offspring will fall in hereditary endowment below the level needed for a fairly human life.

But again the quibblers are active. And again they drag in legislation. Are Nazis in Germany justified in making laws to sterilise the Jews? Are Jews in Palestine justified in agitating for the sterilisation of the Nazis? Since the cleverest people in the community are often the most dangerous, must we not (an ingenious professor suggests) begin by sterilising the more intelligent classes? And since we can never be certain that any couple will procreate defective offspring, is there any justification at all for eugenic sterilisation?

Of course it is easy to answer these quibblers. In the English-speaking countries, at all events, it is rare to find any proposal for compulsory sterilisation. And while there is never a certainty of defective offspring, so terrible may the results be that any right-feeling person will avoid the smallest probability of producing defectives. With growing knowledge of the facts of heredity the probability becomes more measurable. On those who are blind to the facts social pressure, without *ad hoc* legislation, will inevitably be brought to bear.

That question is to the front just now. The elaborate *Report of the Departmental Committee on Sterilisation*, lately presented to the British Parliament, has attracted wide attention not only at home but abroad; 'there probably never was a more careful consideration of eugenics from the State's point of view,' says the *New York Times*.

The Brock Committee (as it is termed from its chairman's name) unanimously approves of the sterilisation of defectives and those likely to transmit mental or physical defects, male and female, and it is opposed to this being done in an institution which might discredit the operation. It is agreed that the proceeding must be voluntary. But the Committee demands legislation.

It is generally held, both inside and outside Great Britain, that this demand for legislation will meet with no response. Even the leading English scientific journal, *Nature*, while finding that the report 'heralds a new era,' also remarks that sterilisation in England 'in all probability will not gain the support of the law.' As the Committee went out of its way to repeat, without contradicting, the superstition that sterilisation is at present illegal, it will thus have done its best to kill the measure of social reform which it rightly considers imperative. The Committee itself here sadly displays the human defects it sets out to extirpate!

Yet we may be thankful that this piece of legislation is not likely to come about. Before advocating it the Committee might have taken the trouble to learn something about legislation. Sir Ambrose Fleming has lately pointed out how the history of telegraphy, telephony, electric lighting, and wireless telegraphy has illustrated the evils of premature legislation. Acts were passed to, as it was ironically termed, 'facilitate' these processes, and in reality they nearly throttled them, wrapping them up in endless bandages of red tape which had eventually to be, at all events in part, removed.

Certainly good results in this field are shown by legislation in California. But not only is the American tradition in these matters different from the English, but California here stands almost, though not quite, alone.

Anyone who knows anything of the cautious and timid temper of the conservative English mind in all matters that concern sex could have told the Brock Committee something that the forty-one learned experts called before it evidently knew nothing about; and that is that any law on sterilisation passed by a British Parliament would be so hedged round by qualifications as to be unworkable. What we need is simple. The well-to-do can already secure sterilisation. We want facilities, under medical advice, for those who cannot afford the operation. That could be provided today.

The first step, indeed, may be difficult. All advance in social reform, even when it involves surgery, is, and always has been, effected by heroic pioneers who are ready to act, and even, if need be, to become martyrs. They slowly win the world to their side. The law limps behind.

LXX

CAN WE STANDARDISE LOVE?

I HAVE searched myself all through, and yet can find no false note. Am I completely in two halves? Or is it possible to frankly and quite desperately love two people? During the coming weeks alone I will try to get this clear to myself.'

The writer is a woman, unmarried, who has passed the age of thirty with but little experience of love in her life, though she is of sensitively feminine organisation. Now she is surprised to find herself in love at the same time with two men, men certainly of very unlike characters, yet both attractive to her.

Only yesterday I received a letter from another woman who, in telling me of domestic difficulties with her husband, with whom I am also acquainted, and of her approaching divorce, remarks: 'I know that men are more polygamous than women, and I do not share my husband's views that women are polygamous. Personally I do not feel so, and it seems to me that this is Nature's plan, for which men should be thankful. Of course I know that there are exceptions to Nature's rule.'

To further complicate the problem I also hear from another woman, who has been married, and happily married, but is now a widow. She writes with reference to the conclusions in Soviet Russia of Professor Blonsky, which I have elsewhere summarised, in a comparison of what he calls the poly-erotic woman, the woman who can be attracted to more than one man, with the mono-erotic woman who is only attracted to one man. Blonsky finds that in nearly all general respects and social aptitude the mono-erotic woman is superior to the poly-erotic woman.

My correspondent considers that I have not sufficiently protested against that conclusion which both she and her husband found unjustified. 'The balance seems to me,' she writes, 'in favour of the poly-erotic woman. My own experience, however, has been that the ordinary man, though attracted to the poly-erotic type of woman, marries the mono-erotic type, thereby defeating his own happiness, with the usual unsatisfactory results. That is one of the reasons why we felt it important to uphold the poly-erotic type, or at least give her her due.'

This correspondent is from Scotland, the first two being English. It so happens that a German woman friend, also happily married, had previously written to me in favour of the poly-erotic woman, so nearly in the same sense that I need not quote her words.

So it appears that if we ask ourselves on what pattern Nature has standardised the sexual life of woman we find no agreement. My third correspondent would certainly say that the unhappy situation of the mono-erotic second correspondent supports her argument, but the two would remain opposed in their general rules. And if we increase the number of our random samples we should not clear up the confusion. Neither of the conventional generalisations seems to fit. Men are not always more 'polygamous,' as we incorrectly term it, than women, and the sexes are not always, as the moralist insists they should be, on an equal level and with the same standard. Nature's rule has to give way to Nature's facts.

To me, however, the confusion is more apparent than real. It is due to our mistaken insistence on impressing a rigid law upon Nature. The facts refuse to fit the law, for the simple reason that the facts are all different even when they approximate to the same pattern. No two leaves on a tree are identical in shape. Why should we expect the shape of two souls to be identical? What we see, here as elsewhere in Nature, is a curve of variations, with many shapes of rather similar kind in the centre, with fewer and fewer tapering down on each side towards the abnormal.

Let us render unto Cæsar the things that are Cæsar's. That is to say, in terms of today, let us standardise the things that admit of standardisation. But it is hopeless to attempt to standardise love.

LXXI

WHAT IS HAPPINESS?

ALL my best wishes for your continued happiness.' That formula enters into so many letters one receives that I suppose I ought long ago to have accepted it as satisfactory. But I have an unfortunate habit of looking conventions in the face and have never been able to overcome a feeling of discomfort in encountering this one. It seems so out of relation with anything I feel, or am entitled to feel, in the world wherein I live. I do not exactly resent a wish so amiably intended. But I smile.

What is 'happiness'? If we consult the Dictionary we find that 'happy' comes from 'hap' — that is to say, chance or luck, something entirely outside one's own responsibility — and that it has come to mean either 'the enjoyment of pleasure without pain' or 'a state in which all desires are satisfied.' That is to say that 'happiness' is either something which is highly undesirable or something which is absolutely impossible.

I sometimes see it stated that there is a 'natural impulse to happiness' which civilisation thwarts. But one does not easily find 'happiness' in Nature. The more carefully we examine animals in Nature, the more impressed we must be by the dangers of their life and the state of fear and anxiety in which they live. On that perpetual background, indeed, there are many moments of delight and gratification, of what in ourselves we might term joy. But that is not what is meant by 'happiness.' And it is not civilisation which here thwarts happiness; it is Nature.

Where shall we find what we can call 'happiness'? A careful observer of animal life in captivity in a recent essay entitled 'Behind the Bars,' has argued that the wild animals in the London Zoo are here enabled to live a life of happy contentment impossible under their native conditions. The main instincts of feeding and mating are gratified without any of the risks and dangers they encounter in a wild life, and they are free to enjoy, and do enjoy, all the little distractions which come within the reach of their cages. Although such an existence is not in every respect identical with our civilised human life, it is our ideal; it is what we mean by 'happiness.' It is the safe, comfortable, contented, cheerful, interested life which my friends have in mind when they wish me 'happiness.' I am sure they would be shocked at Mr. Llewellyn Powys's description of this condition as 'a terrible and devastating outrage.'

This matter is really more serious than it may at first appear. That is why I bring it forward. It is largely, though not entirely, because this zoölogical garden pattern of the happy life is so widely accepted, or rather assumed, as the ideal, that we have the spiritual state so common among us today. I mean the state of unrest and discontent, the sense as of a world collapsing in chaos, which so many find disquieting. It is the state of mind of people who have been brought up to regard the world as naturally the abode of 'happiness,' and feel entitled to be aggrieved when they find that it is not.

The same state of mind accounts for the fascination of Bolshevism. There in Russia they are introducing 'happiness,' a vast zoölogical garden where everyone (provided he accepts the Bolshevist faith) is to be guaranteed feeding and mating and the spectacle (carefully expurgated) of amusements brought before the bars of every cage. No more need of religions (except Leninism), since a Heaven of solid and material 'happiness' is to be set up here and now. At all events we are to cherish the faith that it will be. For I read today that the unemployed through no fault of their own are rapidly increasing in Soviet Russia at the moment, and, as there is no provision for them, they have to choose between stealing and starving and meanwhile are doing both.

The world of 'happiness' is not the world that I live in or have ever desired to live in. I can well understand the remark of Goethe in old age that he had had no more than a fortnight's 'happiness' in his life. Yet that long life had been marvellously rich in various labours, and full of human sorrows and human joys. If indeed one has lived among real human beings, suffering and struggling and aspiring, and is one of them oneself, sharing their griefs and their delights, standing up to difficulties, accepting adventure and facing the awful risks, what has one to do with the 'happiness' of the pigsty?

Whether of the pigsty type or of the modern fashionable zoölogical garden type, that 'happiness' has always seemed remote from my world, and indeed from the world, with its endless questions, in which most of us live today. But if that world offers few opportunities to be 'happy,' it offers many to be heroic.

'With all my best wishes for your happiness.' I think it might indicate a finer insight into the nature of ordinary life if we substituted the formula: 'With my best wishes for your heroism.'

THE END

DATE DUE